# Planning and Managing Higher Education Facilities

Harvey H. Kaiser, *Editor*
*Syracuse University*

**NEW DIRECTIONS FOR INSTITUTIONAL RESEARCH**
PATRICK T. TERENZINI, *Editor-in-Chief*
*University of Georgia*

MARVIN W. PETERSON, *Associate Editor*
*University of Michigan*

Number 61, Spring 1989

Paperback sourcebooks in
The Jossey-Bass Higher Education Series

Jossey-Bass Inc., Publishers
San Francisco • London

Harvey H. Kaiser (ed.).
*Planning and Managing Higher Education Facilities.*
New Directions for Institutional Research, no. 61.
Volume XVI, Number 1.
San Francisco: Jossey-Bass, 1989.

*New Directions for Institutional Research*
Patrick T. Terenzini, *Editor-in-Chief*
Marvin W. Peterson, *Associate Editor*

*New Directions for Institutional Research* is published quarterly by
Jossey-Bass Inc., Publishers (publication number USPS 098-830), and
is sponsored by the Association for Institutional Research. The
volume and issue numbers above are included for the convenience of
libraries. Second-class postage paid at San Francisco, California, and
at additional mailing offices. POSTMASTER: Send address changes
to Jossey-Bass Inc., Publishers, 350 Sansome Street, San Francisco,
California 94104.

**Editorial correspondence** should be sent to the Editor-in-Chief,
Patrick T. Terenzini, Institute of Higher Education, University of
Georgia, Athens, Georgia 30602.

Library of Congress Catalog Card Number LC 85-645339

International Standard Serial Number ISSN 0271-0579

International Standard Book Number ISBN 1-55542-868-1

Cover art by WILLI BAUM

Manufactured in the United States of America. Printed on acid-free paper.

# Ordering Information

The paperback sourcebooks listed below are published quarterly and can be ordered either by subscription or single copy.

Subscriptions cost $52.00 per year for institutions, agencies, and libraries. Individuals can subscribe at the special rate of $39.00 per year *if payment is by personal check.* (Note that the full rate of $52.00 applies if payment is by institutional check, even if the subscription is designated for an individual.) Standing orders are accepted.

Single copies are available at $12.95 when payment accompanies order. (California, New Jersey, New York, and Washington, D.C., residents please include appropriate sales tax.) For billed orders, cost per copy is $12.95 plus postage and handling.

Substantial discounts are offered to organizations and individuals wishing to purchase bulk quantities of Jossey-Bass sourcebooks. Please inquire.

Please note that these prices are for the calendar year 1989 and are subject to change without notice. Also, some titles may be out of print and therefore not available for sale.

To ensure correct and prompt delivery, all orders must give either the *name of an individual* or an *official purchase order number.* Please submit your order as follows:

*Subscriptions:* specify series and year subscription is to begin.
*Single Copies:* specify sourcebook code (such as, IR1) and first two words of title.

Mail orders for United States and Possessions, Latin America, Canada, Japan, Australia, and New Zealand to:
Jossey-Bass Inc., Publishers
350 Sansome Street
San Francisco, California 94104

Mail orders for all other parts of the world to:
Jossey-Bass Limited
28 Banner Street
London EC1Y 8QE

*New Directions for Institutional Research Series*
Patrick T. Terenzini *Editor-in-Chief*
Marvin W. Peterson, *Associate Editor*

# Contents

# Editor's Notes

The growth of campus physical resources as a major component of capital assets, concern for the condition of physical plants, and the rising cost of maintenance and operations have focused attention on how campuses manage facilities. Despite these developments, *New Directions for Institutional Research* has never published a volume on facilities. This sourcebook has been prepared to provide information on facilities management for institutional researchers.

The response to institutional concerns about facilities has produced a trend toward the consolidation of facilities-related activities into a single, comprehensive organization. A new field is evolving, along with innovative organizational structures and information needs. Administrators engaged in these activities tend to be operations oriented and spend little time theorizing on concepts. The available literature is scarce and typically oriented to specific management issues.

It is fortunate that the authors represented in this volume, who have been involved in various aspects of facilities management, reflect on the why, what, and how of the way they do their jobs. Each chapter is enriched by theories and applications, and the topics addressed in the chapters evolve in a sequence that moves from a global perspective to specific issues. Of course, each chapter can be read independently.

The topics in this sourcebook cover three areas: The first two chapters define facilities management and a planning process that is capable of integrating academic, fiscal, and facilities planning. The next four chapters address issues relating to space management, including information collection methods and applications of space planning guidelines. Terms are defined, and valuable background material on the broad context of facilities management is conveyed. The last two chapters discuss ways of budgeting and financial planning for plant assets.

In Chapter One, William Middleton defines facilities management. The new orientation to comprehensive management of campus physical resources is viewed as resulting principally from financial considerations. This and other motives to make efficient use of funds and staff in meeting campus missions are illustrated by trends of the past decade in three areas: facilities planning and acquisition, facilities maintenance and operations, and facilities assignment and utilization. In Chapter Two, Donald Bruegman outlines a process for integrating academic, fiscal, and facilities planning into an effective overall campus planning process. The process, which begins with a statement on institutional priorities, is described, and nine criteria to guide the development of a successfully integrated program are articulated.

1

The next four chapters provide a comprehensive overview of space management that can serve as a resource on that subject for institutional researchers. Daniel Montgomery's chapter on organizing for space management examines several facets of the topic and instructs on critical points. He examines ten trends related to space management in higher education and describes some appropriate strategies for management responses. The chapter provides a model for exploring trends affecting space management and contains pointers for implementing space management programs.

Kreon Cyros describes an innovative method for inventorying space in Chapter Four. The INSITE system developed by the author at the Massachusetts Institute of Technology can serve as a model for facilities allocations, operations, and planning at any large institution. Furthermore, the INSITE system concept of sharing information through a consortium of users has gained widespread acceptance.

Space management relies on accurate inventories and practices for planning and evaluating space usage. In Chapter Five, Jack Probasco provides background on the development of space planning guidelines. He examines criteria for a variety of functional types of space: classrooms, laboratories, offices, libraries, and general and special uses.

Dogmatic use of space planning guidelines is a pitfall in the application of any set of standards. In Chapter Six, Gail Milgrom and Elizabeth Sisam respond to the use of general guidelines at the campus level. They propose a responsive, objective process of space analysis that is at once site specific and tailored to use by individual departments. Standardization is protected but not at the expense of an equitable approach to various levels of facilities planning.

The last two chapters examine the financial aspects of facilities management. In Chapter Seven, Laura Saunders explores a major current issue of higher education, budgeting for deferred maintenance. The author draws on her experience in establishing adequate funding levels to describe the process required to develop accurate information, set priorities, and make decisions. In Chapter Eight, Jack Dunn brings the volume full circle by looking at the larger issues of financial planning for plant assets. The author proposes an approach to long-term funding for plant upkeep and renewal.

Preparation of this volume has offered me an opportunity to explore concepts with articulate practitioners in the field of facilities management. It is hoped that these articles, taken individually or collectively, will inspire institutional researchers to examine their relationships to this rapidly evolving field of higher education. I am especially appreciative of the authors' efforts to formulate their ideas and experiences in chapters that make valuable contributions to the literature on their subjects.

I want to acknowledge the initiative of the Association of Institutional Research Publications Board in suggesting the preparation of this volume. Pat Terenzini, editor-in-chief for the *New Directions for Institutional Research* series, was especially helpful in guiding the volume's development and in making suggestions on content.

Harvey H. Kaiser
Editor

*Harvey H. Kaiser is senior vice-president for facilities administration at Syracuse University. He has written extensively on the subject of facilities management and consulted internationally for higher education, governments, and private corporations.*

*Physical facilities represent a substantial investment for any institution of higher education, and the costs for maintenance and operation of plant represent a sizable part of the annual operating budget. Higher education is moving toward an increasingly comprehensive form of facilities management to assure that this investment is adequately preserved and effectively utilized.*

# Comprehensive Facilities Management

## William D. Middleton

Aside from financial management itself, the management of facilities has become what is commonly the largest of all the nonacademic support functions of higher education. The size of the facilities inventory; the cost of its acquisition, maintenance, and operation; and its technical complexity are all growing at a rapid rate.

Currently, the U.S. investment in higher education plant represents a replacement value estimated at over $300 billion, (based on data developed by the national survey of capital renewal and deferred maintenance costs sponsored by the Association of Physical Plant Administrators of Colleges and Universities [APPA], the National Association of Colleges and University Business Officers [NACUBO], and Coopers & Lybrand [1989]), and for the 1987-88 academic year its annual maintenance and operating costs are estimated to be in excess of $8 billion (based on 1985-86 data from the Center for Statistics, U.S. Department of Education, projected to 1987-88 by APPA). Annual investment in new or renovated facilities was estimated at $15.8 billion during the 1987-88 academic year.

In its broadest sense, facilities management in higher education may be thought of as a triad of functional areas: *planning and acquisition* activities related to the planning, design, and construction of the facilities required to support teaching, research, and public service functions; the

H. H. Kaiser (ed.). *Planning and Managing Higher Education Facilities.*
New Directions for Institutional Research, no. 61. San Francisco: Jossey-Bass, Spring 1989.

*maintenance and operation* of facilities; and the *assignment and utilization* of facilities.

Underlying the importance of each of these facilities management functional areas are the substantial financial needs of facilities acquisition, maintenance, and operation.

Traditionally, institutions of higher education generally function in these three broad areas in a loosely decentralized manner. For example, the process of facilities planning and acquisition is quite often carried out by a facilities planning and construction office or similar unit whose activities are confined to this function alone. Maintenance and repair, minor renovations, and the provision of utilities services are usually the responsibility of an independent buildings and grounds or physical plant department. Management of the process of facilities assignment and utilization is most often done by still another organizational unit, typically a staff function in the college or university administration. Generally, the financial responsibilities of these units are confined to budgeting and expenditure management; major financial concerns are left to the institution's business officer.

While the triad of facilities management functions is most often carried out on this decentralized basis, compelling arguments can be made for a more comprehensive approach to facilities management. With the constantly shifting patterns of institutional organization that characterize most institutions of higher education, it is usually difficult to identify any clear-cut trends or directions in organizational concepts. Nevertheless, in recent years there has been a detectable though modest movement in the direction of a more comprehensive approach to facilities management, under which the full range of facilities management functions is carried out by a comprehensive organization headed by a broad-based facilities management professional.

**Trends and Issues**

Several major considerations are driving the trend toward a comprehensive facilities organization and reliance on more highly qualified—and diverse—facilities managers: rapidly increasing costs for the acquisition of new facilities, a substantial backlog of unfunded deferred maintenance and capital renewal needs, rising maintenance and operating costs, and the growing complexity of college and university facilities.

*Increasing Acquisition Costs.* One of the most urgent considerations driving institutions toward improved and innovative facilities management is the sharply increasing acquisition costs for the new facilities required to support ever more complex higher education activities. The utilization of already existing facilities assets must be maximized in order to limit the scope of new facilities acquisitions. Rigorous space utilization standards must be applied, and carefully developed design standards must provide the lowest feasible initial acquisition and life cycle ownership costs. Confronted with high acquisition costs, institutions are increasingly employing innovative facilities financing, long-term leasing, and other new financial strategies. Increasingly, too, colleges and universities are becoming active rather than passive players in real property development.

*Rising Operating and Maintenance Costs.* Sharply increasing operating and maintenance costs are also placing heavy demands on the resourcefulness of facilities managers. Adding to the difficulty of this task is an enormous burden of deferred maintenance and unmet capital renewal needs developed over several decades of rapid growth in higher education, when resources were concentrated not on the maintenance and modernization of old facilities but on the acquisition of new buildings. The 1988 national survey of deferred maintenance and capital renewal needs in U.S. colleges and universities (Association of Physical Plant Administrators . . . , 1989) found that $60 to $70 billion may be required to meet all current needs. More than $20 billion of this requirement represents urgent needs.

Adding to maintenance needs were the enormous increases in energy costs of the 1970s, which further limited the funding available for basic maintenance and repair of facilities. While the rate of increase in energy costs moderated in the late 1970s and 1980s, these costs are beginning to rise sharply again, and this trend can be expected to continue into the 1990s.

### Facilities Complexity

Yet another trend that is adding to both the difficulty and the cost of the facilities management function is the growing complexity in the facilities required to meet the needs of modern education, research, and health care. Increasingly complex and sophisticated equipment and systems are being required in such areas as environmental control, utilities services, communications and data transmission, and central energy control. These requirements affect facilities acquisition costs. Table 1 compares budgeted facility construction costs for modern educational buildings in 1988 with equivalent figures of a decade earlier.

In addition to its impact on initial acquisition costs, the multiplying effect of facilities complexity carries over equally to facilities maintenance and operating costs. For example, the maintenance and energy costs for a sophisticated modern laboratory building can run as much as 100 to 250 percent over the costs for a typical academic building, despite all the gains that have been made in energy-efficient buildings and systems. Complexity can equally affect the character of the required maintenance

**Table 1. Higher Education Construction Costs, 1978 and 1988**

|  | 1988 Costs[a] | 1978 Costs[b] |
|---|---|---|
|  | *(in dollars per gross square foot)* | |
| Classroom and faculty office building | $107 | $77 |
| Medical research building | $132 | $120 |
| Tertiary care teaching hospital | $212 | $96 |

[a] Current actual or estimated construction costs for projects at the University of Virginia, Charlottesville, adjusted for inflation to mid 1988.

[b] Average costs for comparable projects at other locations adjusted for inflation to mid 1978 and by area differentials to Charlottesville equivalent cost.

force, necessitating both a highly qualified staff and continuing training and development programs to develop and maintain the required skill levels.

## The Facilities Management Triad

Increasingly, institutions of higher education are moving toward the development of facilities management organizations with broad technical and managerial capabilities that treat the management of facilities in a much more comprehensive and integral way. Before we examine this trend, we need to review the normal range of functions within each functional area of the triad.

*Facilities Planning and Acquisition.* The facilities planning and acquisition functional area is concerned with overall facilities master planning for an institution, capital project planning and programming, architectural and engineering design for new or renovated facilities or for major maintenance and repair projects, and construction contract administration. These activities are most often conducted by a separate organization unit, but, depending on the scope of an institution's overall facilities program, they are sometimes combined with either the facilities and space assignment and utilization function or with the facilities maintenance and operations function.

*Facilities Maintenance and Operations.* The facilities maintenance and operations functional area is concerned with facilities inspection programs, maintenance program planning and budgeting, maintenance workload management, preventive and routine maintenance and major facilities maintenance repair, facilities renovations, such maintenance services as custodial and grounds care, utilities services generation and distribution, communication services, transportation services, and other support services. These functions are typically provided by a physical plant or buildings and grounds department.

*Facilities Assignment and Utilization.* The facilities assignment and utilization functional area is concerned with the maintenance of an institution's detailed facilities space inventory data, the monitoring and reporting of facilities utilization, and the assignment and reassignment of facilities and space to specific functional units based upon established space utilization standards and criteria. It may also be concerned with management of real estate. It is in this last area of facilities assignment and utilization that some real leverage may exist over the total cost of owning, maintaining, and operating facilities in a college or university.

To gain some understanding of the potential facilities program cost savings that can be achieved through effective assignment and utilization, we might begin by quantifying the approximate annual cost of owning, maintaining, and operating typical college or university facilities. Table 2 shows annual cost figures for a large state university in the southeast. These figures are based upon actual maintenance and operating cost experience. Acquisition costs are expressed as an annualized cost based upon a thirty-year fixed-rate mortgage.

From the data in Table 2, we can calculate that the total annual cost of owning and operating a 120-square-foot faculty office is $2,200 per year. For a 500-square-foot laboratory space, the cost is $15,000 per year, and for a 2000-square-foot auditorium, it is $36,000 per year.

How can these costs be controlled? Cost-effective design or efficient maintenance programs can produce marginal percentage reductions in virtually all these costs. Effective utilization of existing space can reduce the need for acquiring additional facilities. Thus it is possible to eliminate costs for additional facilities.

Table 2. Higher Education Annualized Facility Acquisition,
Maintenance, and Operating Cost

| | *Annual Cost* |
|---|---|
| *Academic Building* | *(in dollars per assignable square foot)* |
| Acquisition cost | $15.52/ASF |
| Maintenance cost | 0.56/ASF |
| Custodial cost | 0.67/ASF |
| Utilities cost | 1.43/ASF |
| Total: | $18.18/ASF/Year |
| | |
| *Research Building* | |
| Acquisition cost | $26.11/ASF |
| Maintenance cost | 0.83/ASF |
| Custodial cost | 0.63/ASF |
| Utilities cost | 0.57/ASF |
| Total | $30.14/ASF/Year |

## The Concept of Comprehensive Facilities Management

There are some important relationships among the functional areas of the facilities management triad that argue for a close relationship among all three. For example, a close link between the assignment and utilization function and the facilities planning and acquisition process is essential to assure that any programming for new facilities is based upon real need. A careful analysis of the existing facilities inventory against a projection of requirements based upon accepted space criteria and standards is an essential part of an effective facilities planning process. As facilities become ever more complex, a close and continuing dialogue between those who plan and those who maintain and operate facilities becomes increasingly important. Such a dialogue assures that both the maintainability lessons learned by the maintenance and operating forces about specific materials and equipment and the specific design requirements for efficient maintenance and operations can be incorporated into plans and specifications for new construction. Finally, a close relationship between the staff involved in facilities assignment and utilization and the staff involved in maintenance can help to focus limited maintenance resources on the areas of highest utilization or greatest need.

For all these reasons, there is a general trend toward the development of comprehensive, full-service facilities management organizations in higher education. In such organizations, all three functional areas are integrated into a single overall facilities management organization, usually headed by a broad-based facilities management professional. Increasingly, institutions of higher education are establishing senior facilities administrator positions that encompass this full range of facilities management responsibilities. At a limited but growing number of institutions, these facilities management positions are being established at the vice-presidential level. The kind of facilities manager and organization increasingly being sought was described in these terms by a large western public university in a recent *Chronicle of Higher Education* position advertisement:

> **Vice-Chancellor, Facilities.** The Vice-Chancellor, Facilities, a new position, will be the campus's senior officer for development, construction, and management of all capital facilities and associated physical environments on the campus. Responsibilities include architectural and engineering programming, design, and quality control; management of facilities construction and renovation; maintenance of the facilities and the physical environments; and development and facilitation of the entrepreneurial programs and financing relating to capital projects. The Vice-Chancellor reports directly to the Chancellor. Qualifications include a record of demonstrated accomplishment in facilities development and

management in a setting equivalent to that of a large research university, excellent human relations skills, demonstrable creativity and effectiveness, sensitivity to environmental and social issues, and the ability to communicate effectively orally and in writing. A minimum of five years effective management experience is required. A postbaccalaureate degree in a related area and experience in a university environment are desirable.

One can expect a continuing trend toward the establishment of similar high-level positions with broad, comprehensive facilities management responsibilities as colleges and universities confront the need for strengthened facilities programs in the future.

## Conclusions

For institutions of higher education, the broad area of facilities management is becoming increasingly important. This is almost inevitable as colleges and universities begin to come to grips with the realities of their enormous backlog of deferred maintenance and capital renewal needs; the demand for the increasingly complex and costly facilities required to support modern programs of teaching, research, and health care; and the rapidly rising maintenance and operating costs required to support these maintenance- and energy-intensive facilities. As higher education administrators recognize the value of close and continuing relationships between all elements of a facilities management program, the concept of comprehensive facilities management organizational structures can be expected to become increasingly common. For facilities management professionals, this should represent both an opportunity and a need to expand their managerial skills.

For institutional researchers, the heightened interest in facilities management will have important implications. We can expect the demand for good standard and comparative data concerning facilities assignment and utilization to increase as colleges and universities try to increase the productivity of their facilities assets. The identification and quantification of requirements for capital renewal and deferred maintenance funding will have new importance. Interest in the development of standard and comparative data expenditures for facilities maintenance and operation should also increase.

## References

Association of Physical Plant Administrators of Colleges and Universities, National Association of Colleges and University Business Officers, and Coopers & Lybrand. *The Decaying American Campus: A Ticking Time Bomb*. Alexandria, Va.: Association of Physical Plant Administrators of Colleges and Universities, 1989.

*William D. Middleton is assistant vice-president for physical plant at the University of Virginia. He has responsibility for space administration, facilities planning and construction, and facilities maintenance and operations for the university's academic division and health sciences center, including the University of Virginia Hospitals.*

*The five principal products of an integrated academic, fiscal, and facility planning process are an academic plan, a physical development plan, institutional priorities, a capital budget plan, and an operating budget plan.*

# An Integrated Approach to Academic, Fiscal, and Facility Planning

*Donald C. Bruegman*

A truly effective planning process integrates academic, fiscal, and facility planning. This can be accomplished through preparation of the following plans: An academic program plan with a mission statement and goals for the future, a long-range plan for land and building use, a strategic plan defining institutional priorities for the planning period, a capital budget plan, and a biennial operating budget plan allocating dollars to programs that can be translated into an annual revenue and expenditure budget.

This chapter describes each of these five plans in detail. It offers criteria for successful implementation of a planning process that integrates these five plans.

## Products of the Planning Process

As just stated, the five principal products of an integrated academic, fiscal, and facility planning process are an academic plan, a physical development plan, institutional priorities, a capital budget plan, and an operating budget plan.

H. H. Kaiser (ed.). *Planning and Managing Higher Education Facilities.*
New Directions for Institutional Research, no. 61. San Francisco: Jossey-Bass, Spring 1989.

*Academic Plan.* The academic plan is the foundation of the entire process. Without it, there is no basis for planning. The academic plan is prepared by a faculty committee under the leadership of the chief academic officer. The faculty planning committee is ideally a permanent committee with members rotating on and off the committee every two to three years. In this manner, more members of the faculty are exposed to planning.

Academic planning is a continuous process, and the results can be incorporated into accreditation cycles and used to meet statewide planning requirements. Issues can be addressed on an annual basis. For example, one year can be devoted to general education requirements and the next year to international education or economic development programs. In this way, the academic plan is current, it represents a dynamic product, and it can be available for other uses.

The structure of the academic plan is such that it contains a global mission statement and a set of long-term goals for the institution. This is a reasonable expectation for a plan developed by a faculty committee with rotating membership. It is the chief academic officer's job to translate the mission and goal statements into an action plan when preparing the institutional priorities.

*Physical Development Plan.* The physical development plan is far more specific than a landscape or building site plan. The physical development plan is program driven. It needs to assess the spatial needs of academic and support programs. Program requirements need to be quantified in terms of the amount of square feet needed for classroom space, laboratory space, office space, physical and recreational space, and other appropriate categories of space. Program-related space standards need to be applied to each space category based on the student, faculty, and staff population and then compared to existing space assignments. If necessary, space allocations for existing programs may have to be realigned.

The use of consultants to develop a physical development plan provides an objective, external point of view. A campus officer with appropriate authority and responsibility must manage the consultants' activities with participation from a steering committee or task force composed of representatives of the programs for which space allocations are being planned. The president should interact often enough with the consultants to assure that they do not drift off course.

Once a physical development plan is in place, capital planning can become routine. Priorities for construction and renovation projects can be set as part of the institutional priorities' planning process.

*Institutional Priorities.* Institutional priorities should be thought of as the institution's strategic plan. Today, the development of such priorities is sometimes referred to as *issue management.* The setting of institutional priorities is best accomplished on a biennial basis, with all priorities being reevaluated every two years.

The statement of institutional priorities contains a more elaborate mission statement and expands on the goals in the academic plan. During this stage of the planning process, a set of objectives is developed for accomplishing each goal. Each objective then has its own set of strategies and tasks for carrying out the objective. In this manner, goals are translated into objectives, objectives into strategies, and strategies into tasks. By breaking goals down in this manner, one can establish an implementation plan and fix responsibility for execution (Bruegman, 1984).

Institutional priorities are a product of a campus-wide committee composed of faculty, administrators, and students. The committee should be chaired by an administrator, since the ultimate responsibility for implementation resides with the administration. The charge to the committee overseeing the preparation of institutional priorities should be clear. It is the committee's job to review and ratify priorities, not to conceive them. The administrative officers—vice-presidents, deans, and directors—who are responsible for the programs to which the goals relate are the ones who determine what objectives, strategies and tasks will be included in the statement of institutional priorities. Administrative officers, through consultation with their appropriate faculty and staff, are best qualified to conceive the priorities.

Once institutional priorities are in place, they should be ranked in order of importance so that preparation of the capital and operating budget plans can become routine.

*Capital and Operating Budget Plans.* Capital and operating budget plans are derived from the institutional priorities. Like the institutional priorities, these plans are prepared by the administration in consultation with appropriate governance groups within the institutions. Both the capital and the operating budget planning cycles should be synchronized with the two-year time period covered by the institutional priorities.

The major difference between the institutional priorities and the capital and operating budget plans is that the capital and operating budget plans are constrained by the availability of resources. Up to this point in the planning process, resource availability has not been a major factor. Now it is. However, if the institutional priorities have been ranked in order of importance, preparation of the capital and operating budget plans is much easier. Failure to rank order the institutional priorities requires prioritizing programs during this step in the process. In order not to become bogged down at this stage of the process and in order not to allow resource constraints to alter priorities, planners should rank priorities at the time when the institutional priorities are prepared.

The operating budget plan should not be confused with the line-item annual budget. The annual budget is the traditional line-item budget that is used to control revenue and expenditures. It is prepared after the biennial budget plan has been approved. The biennial budget plan is usually developed on an incremental or decremental basis, depending upon the availability of resources. Funds are allocated in accordance with the institutional priorities.

It is important to include all fund sources when the capital and operating budget plans are prepared. All too often, especially in large institutions with multiple off-budget fund sources, plans are based only on recurring revenue sources, such as state approriations, tuition revenue, and other traditional sources of educational and general revenue. Sound budget planning takes into consideration all fund sources, including the unrestricted and restricted fund balances traditionally managed as departmental funds.

## Integrating the Process

Integrating the planning processes described in this chapter is like learning to drive an automobile that has a standard transmission with five forward gears. The process does not always work smoothly in the beginning. Sometimes, you skip a step, or the transition from one step to another is not smooth but abrupt. But, as you gain experience, the outcomes improve. Even though the process may not be perfect throughout every planning cycle, you still move the institution forward.

The most important step in the entire process is the preparation of the statement of institutional priorities. It links academic program planning with fiscal planning and thus improves the chances for full integration of the planning process.

The statement of institutional priorities expresses an institution's mission, goals, and objectives in very specific terms. Such a statement identifies the priorities for program development. A statement on institutional priorities can include an institutional planning statement and sections on planning assumptions, goals and objectives, and implementation strategies.

*Institutional Planning Statement.* The statement of institutional priorities opens with an institutional planning statement. This section elaborates on the institution's global mission statement from the academic plan. An institutional planning statement is specific, up to date, and to the point. It recognizes that the institution cannot be all things to all people. What it says sets the tone for the entire planning process. It contains statements like the following:

- The university shall enhance the quality of its strong programs and strive to improve other selected programs.
- The university serves the state and, because of its geographic location, preferentially serves the metropolitan area in which it is located.
- The university's future role will be demonstrated by guiding growth in selected programs and de-emphasizing programs which would be offered elsewhere or for which there is inadequate demand.

*Planning Assumptions.* The second section of the statement of institutional priorities is devoted to planning assumptions. Planning assumptions are expressed in terms of financial constraints, demographic and enrollment considerations, and institutional program directions. Financial constraints and demographic and enrollment considerations need little explanation. They consist of real-world expectations and describe the institution's planning environment. Here are some examples of meaningful assumptions:

- Revenues will not permit all existing programs to continue at their current level of funding.
- Prospective student admissions will be influenced by an institutional response to the following four issues: Students have an interest in a more career-oriented curriculum. Enrollments in medicine and dentistry will decline. Interest in high technology programs is increasing. The need for qualified elementary and secondary school teachers will increase.

Statements about the direction in which the institution is heading complete this section. For example, will the institution be a comprehensive, research, or doctoral-granting institution? Will the institution grow or contract? Will support services be enhanced or diminished? Will public service programs be self-supporting? These are just a few of the questions that must be answered as one develops institutional program plans. The more specific these plans are, the easier it is to develop the goals and objectives that follow.

*Goals and Objectives.* Goals and objectives need no introduction to those familiar with planning. In the context of the statement on institutional priorities, goals are general statements of intent and look at least six to eight years into the future. If the academic plan has been prepared properly, the goals that it contains can be restated here. However, at this stage of the planning process, goal statements usually need to be reworded so that they are more explicit. Objectives relate to a specific goal and indicate how the goal will be achieved. Objectives are expected to be accomplished in less time, usually four to six years. In the statement on institutional priorities, goals and objectives are best categorized under the following program headings: instruction, research, public service, support services, student financial assistance, and auxiliary enterprises. Here is an example of an instructional goal statement and its supporting objectives:

*Goal:* Attract and retain productive faculty by providing both monetary and nonmonetary incentives that reward quality academic contributions and aid in the adjustment to changing university needs.

*Objective 1:* Strive to bring faculty salary averages up to levels prevailing nationally in peer institutions.

*Objective 2:* Devise a salary and reward structure that will improve incentives for faculty excellence.

*Objective 3:* Assure that quality instruction is given an appropriate emphasis in the faculty reward system.

*Objective 4:* Provide new options for faculty affected by changing university needs.

*Objective 5:* Increase the number of minority faculty eligible for tenure.

*Implementation Strategies.* This final section of the statement on institutional priorities is a further elaboration of the goals and objectives. Just as each goal has its supporting objectives, each objective has its supporting strategies. Strategies relate to the immediate future and are intended to be implemented during the upcoming planning cycle, which is usually two years. Because of the short time span for implementation, strategies are reflective of the current fiscal and economic environment described under the planning assumptions. During periods of economic stress, strategies are likely to focus on retrenchment and the reallocation of resources. As the economy becomes more favorable, strategies may begin to deal with controlled expansion and development. Here is an example of the strategies related to objectives in the preceding section:

*Objective 2:* Devise a salary and reward structure that will improve incentives for faculty excellence.

*Strategy 1:* Retain and reward faculty on the basis of merit.

*Strategy 2:* Require comprehensive annual reviews of performance of all faculty.

*Strategy 3:* Continue and expand the University Convocation and Distinguished Faculty Awards Program.

*Strategy 4:* Devise ways of recognizing special faculty achievements and contributions.

*Strategy 5:* Refine the posttenure review system.

One university's statement on institutional priorities is twenty-seven pages long. It contains twelve goals, thirty-seven objectives and one hundred and nine strategies. The essence of the document is its strategies. Strategies state the priorities for the upcoming biennium. They need to be rank ordered. The strategies give the planning process meaning and vitality.

## Criteria for Success

Nine criteria are essential for successful integration of academic, fiscal, and facility planning: a comprehensive planning process, a team-oriented organizational structure, skilled technical staff, an information base, use of external consultants, controlled participatory involvement, decisive leadership, governing board involvement, and fixed responsibility for implementation.

*Comprehensive Planning Process.* Planning must be an ongoing process. There must be a strong commitment to planning regardless of the level of planning sophistication among the organizational units. University publications must keep the planning process and the outcomes of this process in view, and the process and its outcomes must be promoted both inside and outside the institution. Everyone must be aware that there is an ongoing planning process and that a specific plan is in place.

*Team-Oriented Organizational Structure.* The process must be built upon an organizational structure that allows negotiation and compromise. Shared management responsibility is extremely important, and the ability of the vice-presidents to interact and cooperate with one another is of paramount importance.

*Skilled Technical Staff.* A strong and diverse technical staff is an absolute necessity. This staff includes architects, engineers, accountants, and data processing personnel. An institutional research office is well suited to coordinate the overall planning process, but strong staff support will be needed throughout the organization.

*Information Base.* Automated systems containing a data base with space, personnel, financial, and enrollment data should be in place. The ability to access and merge these data provides the information base necessary for planning.

*Use of External Consultants.* Consultants do not make the process work. That is the institution's job. However, consultants can be helpful in preparing a physical development plan and in financial analysis and program evaluation. Consultants are good at assessing needs, proposing and evaluating alternatives, and recommending choices for consideration and implementation.

*Controlled Participatory Involvement.* Knowing how to orchestrate participatory involvement throughout the process is a key factor. For example, the academic plan is best prepared by a faculty committee under the leadership of the chief academic officer. Institutional priorities and physical development plans should be the products of university advisory committees composed of faculty, administrators, and students. The capital and operating budget plans are prepared by the administration in consultation with appropriate governance groups. All plans are subject to final approval by the president and the governing board.

*Decisive Leadership.* Strong involvement and support from the president is essential. In addition, the administration must maintain control of the process and balance participatory involvement to assure that governance groups support the outcomes. Without decisive leadership on the part of all administrative officers, the process will drift, and the plan will be nothing more than a set of unrealistic expectations.

*Governing Board Involvement.* At key decision-making points along the way, the governing board must be involved. Most important, it must approve the mission and goal statements. Waiting until a plan is in place before seeking approval from the governing board is ill-advised and can render the plan ineffective and meaningless.

*Fixed Responsibility for Implementation.* One person, either the chief academic officer or the chief administrative officer, should be in charge of the entire process. Responsibility for implementation of planning outcomes must rest with the appropriate vice-presidents. To permit measurement of progress during implementation, outcomes should be quantified wherever possible. It is also important to balance the roles of academic, fiscal, and space planners in the process. In the absence of such an effort, there may well be an imbalance in qualitative and quantitative factors in the plan.

## Summary

Sound planning is necessary if any organization is to be successful. Higher education has experimented with many innovative planning techniques, including planning, programming, budgeting systems (PPBS) and other zero-based budgeting and strategic planning. Success in adapting sophisticated planning techniques to higher education has been limited. Why? The most likely answer is that the products of higher education are altogether different from the products of a private business or government agency. The major products of higher education are an educated person, a research breakthrough, or a public service. Such outcomes are not standardized, and they cannot be quantified by the bottom-line mentality that is so prevalent in society today. Many believe that if something cannot be measured, it is unmanageable.

Yet, in recent years higher education has improved its management skills and strengthened its planning processes. These gains have been made because techniques have been developed to integrate academic, fiscal, and facility planning. This chapter has described one of these techniques.

## Reference

Bruegman, D. C. "Virginia Commonwealth University: A Working Planning and Management Process." Paper presented at the Conference on Higher Education, University of Arizona, November 28, 1984.

*Donald C. Bruegman is senior vice-president for administration at Virginia Commonwealth University.*

*Colleges and universities increasingly recognize that they must manage their space resources just as they manage their equipment, finances, and personnel.*

# Organizing for Space Management

*Daniel A. Montgomery*

There is no such thing as a free space in higher education. The financial costs of space acquisition, maintenance, and operation cannot be denied. Marsh (Marsh and Griffith, 1985) concluded that, for academic space, about $2,000 per student is needed annually. This amount is consistent with Hamer's (1988) reported annual cost of $2,250-$6,250 per employee for corporate facilities. Managing the use of space and getting the best return on capital investment in facilities require management strategies to be as rigorous as those applied to an institution's financial endowment and personnel resources.

Given the increasing costs for planning, building, and maintaining higher educational facilities, organizing for space management is critical. From an institutional planning and research perspective, it is particularly important to base views of space management needs on trend analysis. By examining broad trends related to space management and applying them to local conditions, the institutional planner is better prepared to respond to the challenge of contributing to the future of his or her institution. The management of space for improved utilization is

The author expresses his gratitude to Melanie Besio, Harvey Kaiser, and Pat Terenzini for their editorial assistance.

H. H. Kaiser (ed.). *Planning and Managing Higher Education Facilities.*
New Directions for Institutional Research, no. 61. San Francisco: Jossey-Bass, Spring 1989.

best accomplished within the framework of identified trends and associated strategies.

This chapter is organized around ten current, national trends related to space management in higher education. For illustrative purposes, each trend is related to a situation at the University of Virginia. For each situation, a few possible strategies are presented. These strategies are not limited to the treatment of any given trend.

## Focus on Program Quality and Space Utilization

In response to the increasing cost of space, colleges and universities are giving more attention to the best use of existing facilities. Hamer (1988) reports that facilities costs, including real estate, fixed assets, and support costs, as a percentage of operating costs have risen from 3 to 10 percent in 1965 to 20 to 30 percent in 1985. Academic institutions are focusing on areas of strength and improved use of current space resources.

While maintaining its traditional areas of quality and strength, such as its undergraduate liberal arts program, the University of Virginia is increasing its research efforts. Emphasis is placed on the recruitment and retention of established teachers and researchers. In anticipation that these faculty will require renovated and new space, the university is becoming more engaged in space inventory, analysis, reporting, and management for improved space utilization. A broad-based university committee has been studying methods for making better use of existing space. The study by the space management task force, under the direction of the vice-president for administration, will assist in determining and acquiring space for projected requirements.

An increased emphasis on user health and environmental standards has emerged as a corollary to this trend. A rise in national concern for personal well-being has resulted in an increase in such actions as fitness center development, handicapped access installations, and asbestos management program implementation.

In response to a growing interest in physical fitness, the university recently built an additional recreational facility. It is constructing a new student health center, and it is planning a sports medicine complex. In recognition of environmental concerns, the university is undertaking a major asbestos control and removal project and plans to demolish a "sick" building with air pollution problems that cannot be corrected cost-effectively.

*Develop and Apply Space Standards.* Well-defined, realistic, and meaningful space guidelines are needed for programming, planning, and analysis. Space excesses and deficiencies are determined by comparing state and local guidelines with the space inventory. Space utilization reports can then be generated for internal and external purposes. In the absence of established guidelines, space programming, planning, and analysis can be based on existing conditions. For example, the University of Virginia has an average instructional office of about 140 square feet and overall uses about 300 net square feet of space per student. This amount of space exceeds state guidelines due in part to the university's mission as a research institution. For classroom planning, the state of Virginia offers a sixteen-square-feet-per-student guideline. In contrast, Castaldi (1987) suggests that 18.1 to 21.8 square feet per student might be assigned in classrooms. Space managers must be aware of both traditional and contemporary values and practices. Because space guidelines vary, space managers should also understand the effective application of standards that are appropriate to the institution and to a particular unit or division. Personnel with these characteristics must be actively recruited and retained by organizers for space management.

***Develop a Basis for Future Space Management.*** Planners need to look ahead in the next few years as well as to develop a long-range planning horizon of perhaps ten years. Associated with a focus on enhancing the quality of relatively strong institutional areas, a special effort is needed for improved space utilization. Planners need to assess current space management strengths and weaknesses within a methodology that integrates financial, academic, and facility goals. A team-oriented organization, with shared management responsibility, is recommended for comprehensive space planning. Top administration needs to be involved throughout the process for successful space management, and this involvement should be reflected in the organizational structure. Personnel with team-building and facilitation skills should be actively supported for improved levels of integration and coordination in decision making. As Cavanaugh (1984) reports, the mission of space management is one of coordination and oversight.

### Orientation Toward Participatory Review and Debate

An increase in national expectations that persons will be involved in the decisions that affect them has been accompanied by a rise in communications technologies that give more people access to information. Automated systems for customized reporting of data, generation of alternative scenarios, and evaluation of possible impacts, coupled with an institutional environment that is more open to discussion, have resulted in a notable increase in decision-making participation.

The consequent increase in discussions at all levels assists coordination and integration. The participation may take time, but important dissensions are revealed, space is more likely to be a better fit, and participation itself is an education to those involved. If people affected by a decision feel that they have been part of the decision-making process, they are more apt to implement the solution effectively. As a result, space utilization is more likely to be improved. In addition, those involved will have a better understanding of the need for and methods of space management, and they will thereby become more supportive of space planning and management efforts.

The University of Virginia's recently established space management task force involves more faculty and staff discussion than ever before. Task force members, who represent a full range of administrative units, are examining how space is managed throughout the various units and recommending improvements to the existing system. Intense deliberations have occurred over schemes for more centralized space management and changes in space guidelines. University-wide space policies and practices have been examined, and a report has been made to the vice-presidential planning group, which includes the president. Participation in space management at the department level, whereby representatives review and update their portion of the space inventory, has also increased. A revised space inventory is then made available to provide decision makers with current data and analyses with recommendations.

*Consider the Time Required for Collaboration and Verification.* Because of increased participation by those involved in the space management process, it is important both to plan ahead in order to anticipate actions and their consequences and to develop some quick and highly visible results. Skilled technical staff must maintain accurate space information and compile and distribute reports in a timely manner for controlled participatory involvement. When organizing for space management, planners need to determine fixed responsibilities for maintaining and reporting information as well as for implementing near-term and long-range strategies at all levels of the institution. Figure 1 shows how various offices have primary responsibility for different functions. Such a distribution of responsibility creates a balance with broad participation.

*View Involvement in the Space Management Process as a Means to Reduce Conflicts.* Planners must manage conflict rather than avoid it. Planners help to identify and diagnose the problem. They facilitate the generation of alternative solutions, and they negotiate and implement an effective action. Although some participants may be obstinate and others may be difficult to involve, both decision makers and users must accept solutions in order for successful space management to occur. Planners must be prepared to look at the problem from different perspectives. Organizationally, space management belongs at the interface of academic, fiscal, and facility planning. Planners must also be prepared to look at precedents, both internal and external, and to select and train personnel for their open-mindedness and their interpersonal and organizational skills. Personnel should be selected for their ability to create effective

Figure 1. Space Management Summary Matrix, University of Virginia

| | Land Inv | Bldg/Equip Inv | Room Inv | Util/Classif | Analyses | Facility Audits | Projection | Schematics | Demol & Acquis | Classrm Imprvmnts |
|---|---|---|---|---|---|---|---|---|---|---|
| Office Space Administration | Maintain parcel inv, comprehensive parcel map, and deed file. Eval local tax assessments. | Estab & maintain bldg database. Develop & maint bldg flr/plans. Work w/Risk Mgt to assign bldg values. | Maintain room inv. Report to State, Comptr & Inst Planning and Studies. | Analyze exist/proposed space utilization schemes, recommend improvements/changes. Reclassify space as necessary. | Based on estab. standards, analyze amt, type, use, cond & qual of space for excesses & deficiencies. | Eval facility use, adaptability & expansion. Coord facility audit. Recommend Cap. Renew projects. | Forecast space needs based on acad plan, space avail & space utilization. | Develop program for matching efficient space utilization w/ institutional goals. | Prep demol requests & notify Rep & Control, Real Est & funding agent upon State approval. Eval bldgs for acquis. | Est cost of proposed classrm improv proj. Purchase furn & equip and coord improvement/major maintenance. |
| A&E Services | | | Report changes in function/use/ plans to Space Admin. | Analyze/synth projects, including spatial & func relationships. Devel environmental studies. | Devel & manage proj for site & bldg constr and renov under Cap. Budget Program. | Eval site & bldg cond, inspect for code compliance. | | Develop A&E system options. Analyze costs, coord proj., chk reg compliance. | | Coord classrm constr & renov proj. Prepare cost rpts. |
| Facilities Planning | Coord submittal of comprehensive parcel map to master plan consultant. | | | | | | Coord submittal of space forecasts to master site plan consultant. | Develop conceptual facility locations. Analyze aesthetic space concerns. | | |
| Work Management | | | | | | Coord facil Insp. Eval internal cond for Facil Audit. | | | | Est material & labor costs of painting/ other improvements/ maintenance projects. |
| Institutional Planning & Studies | | Coord report/ proposals to Higher Educ Trust Fund. | | Prepare classrm utilization report. Coord. Univ position, submit to State. | Prepare allowable space & personnel reports related to guide analyses. | | Forecast student, faculty, staff & equip needs for 10 year Acad plan. | | | |
| Comptroller, Reporting and Control | | Maintain property (equip) inv & report to State. | Report discrep btwn room & equip inventories to Space Admin. | | | | | | | |
| Real Estate & Risk Mgt. | Buy and sell property. Notify Space Admin of land holding changes. | Maintain leased bldg inv. Report inv to Space Admin. | | | | | Maintain inv of available lease and purchase options. | | Evaluate property being considered for acquisition. | |
| Registrar | | | Report changes in classrm inv to Space Admin. | Coord classrm sched & recom improvements. | | | | | | Chair Classrm Improve Committee. |
| Summer Session | | | | Recommend improved classrm sched/utiliz. | | | | | | Suggest classrm improvements. |
| VP Health Sciences | | Maintain bldg plans & inv for Health Sciences. | Report Health Sciences' current room inv to Space Admin. | Eval space use & classification. Recommend assignments. | Apply space stand in analysis of rm use. Devel space defic rpts for Cap Out/other proj. | | Forecast needs for Health Sciences. | Mesh Acad plan with current & alternative space use. | Report bldg demol to Space Admin. | Suggest classroom improvements. |
| Assoc Provost for Academic Affairs | | | | Eval space use & classification, recom assignments. | Apply space stand in analysis & prep of defic rpts. | | Forecast space needs for VP&Provost. | Develop concepts for alternative space use. | | Fund & suggest classrm improvements. Recom academic space improvements. |
| Clinch Valley College | Maintain parcel and deed inv. | Maintain bldg inventory. | Maintain room inventory. | Eval space use & classification. | Analyze space excesses & deficiencies | Evaluate bldg condition. | Forecast space needs for CVC. | Devel concepts for alternative space use. | | |

alternatives that others cannot visualize, and staff should be encouraged to establish acceptable, objective criteria for selecting the best alternative solution. The Office of Space Administration at the University of Virginia has developed terms of agreement among recreational and academic users of common open space. When there was conflict between a field-research unit and golf course managers, a description of the problem and an effective solution was agreed upon by those involved.

## Increasingly Decentralized Support Systems

There is fragmentation in most institutional decision making. A balance of power is desirable, and neither space and academic offices nor budget units tend to dominate administrative decisions consistently. For reasons usually related to autonomy, separate institutional parts do not always act in a coordinated fashion. The need for coordinating decisions has increased with the demand for improved space utilization.

The University of Virginia's space management task force is studying the division of labor in space inventorying, analyzing, and reporting and assessing the best means for networking space management personnel. For example, in recognition of the decentralized nature of room scheduling, the task force is recommending that a common data base be established. Such a data base would make it possible for a variety of units, such as the registrar, dean of students, and director of athletics, to review the schedule of academic and public spaces.

The corollary is that the ability to mandate integrated space management is decreasing. The space czar is an endangered species. The shift toward more decentralized support systems has affected space management. As a result, roles related to space management must be clarified to assist the development, execution, and evaluation of the space planning and allocation processes. An understanding of the division of labor increases the probability of integrating space management into institutional planning processes. In addition, space management tools, such as standards, are more likely to be applied uniformly and accepted.

The university's space management task force, in recognition of a decentralized situation, has supported decisions made within vice-presidential jurisdictions. In cases when issues cross vice-presidential boundaries, the task force recommends that the space administrator develop presentations for a decision by the president's vice-presidential planning group.

*Define Relationships Between Space Management and Other Organizational Functions.* Roles and responsibilities related to space management should be defined within institutional priorities. Duties for space inventory maintenance, analyses, and reporting should be clarified in a framework that integrates the academic plan, capital and operating budgets, and the master site plan. The university's space management summary matrix shown in Figure 1 is one tool for assessing the relationship among space management components.

*Help to Reconcile Boundary-Spanning Concerns of the Organization as a Whole.* The increase in participation and networking brings with it an opportunity for increased conflict in space allocation and management and an increased need for negotiation among and within the vice-presidential units. The university's office of space administration has responded to this situation with numerous studies of alternatives and recommendations to decision makers. The office serves neither as a space czar nor as a divine arbiter. Rather, the role of negotiator and facilitator is emphasized. When planners organize for space management in higher education, they should emphasize conflict resolution skills when selecting and training personnel.

## Partnerships in Meeting New Space Needs

The ability of the private sector of the nation's economy to respond to market conditions and the resources and opportunities within the public sector are increasingly being combined. Rapidly changing financial and enrollment conditions make collaborative efforts in higher education particularly attractive. Partnerships in acquiring, developing, and managing space include private real estate foundations, design-build projects, and city-county-university planning agreements.

The university recently established a real estate foundation to respond to building and land investments in support of the University of Virginia. Real estate transactions and space management for academic purposes now partially occur within the private sector. For example, the foundation has bought and renovated buildings for lease to the university. The community, of which the university is part, is satisfied because the foundation's holdings remain in the tax base. University officials are working with community organizations and are getting developments completed, often with time and money savings, by employing design-build firms.

The foundation has also established "incubator" space for new and promising businesses. Perhaps even more important to public-private partnerships, the neighboring county and city planning groups are participating with the university in joint efforts, such as site plan review, neighborhood studies, and comprehensive, long-term plan development.

*Remember That Long-Term Planning Must Also Produce Results Quickly.* Good intentions are not enough for successful comprehensive, long-term planning. Planners need to identify a component that lends itself to some quick, valued, and highly visible results. For example, with clustered or satellite spaces, planners can select and implement a relatively low-cost component that can be used in the near term. The university's office of space administration recently accomplished this by gaining support for the painting of corridors in the university's most heavily used classroom building. Such immediate evidence of planning should, of course, be consistent with long-term capital project development. Space managers should creatively identify manageable components and execute plans in a business-like manner.

*Attract and Sustain Support at Various Levels of Institutional Decision Making.* Planners must identify and support their constituency—representative participants who are advocates for space management and who comprehend broad interrelationships. For example, to gain support for space standards, planners should involve various levels of decision makers at their own institution, at peer institutions, and at state or province governing agencies as early in the guideline review process as possible. Space managers should not only facilitate boundary-spanning conflicts but support early involvement in decision making of people affected by space changes or of participants in conflicting activities.

**Increasingly Proactive Orientation**

Parallel to the national rise in expectations that people are to be involved in making the decisions that affect them, people have become more active in the development and implementation of those decisions. In higher education, people are particularly well skilled in vocalizing their needs and acting accordingly. Colleges and universities are experiencing an increase in the initiation of new programs. This trend is certainly the case in space management.

The University of Virginia has initiated and adopted a facilities audit program that is linked to the capital outlay process. Coordinated by the university space administrator, an audit team reviews significant buildings and assesses them for deficiencies. Starting with facilities more than fifty years old, the space administrator has advanced buildings with the greatest degree of deficiencies to academic and administrative officials for consideration as capital renewal projects. Instead of an ad hoc or incremental approach and fragmented building studies, this audit team process is repeated biennially. Academic objectives can then be balanced with facility needs and financial resources by local and external decision makers.

Recognizing the rising trend of facilities costs over time, public and private institutions are studying and implementing improved space management techniques. Space is viewed as the most permanent resource, and thus it requires long-term attention. Persistence is needed to demonstrate that an institution is serious about space management.

The development of university building values illustrates such persistence. The state's accepted replacement value of University of Virginia facilities was about doubled over a recent four-year period, with a commensurate increase in funding as a result of the joint efforts of campus physical plant and state officials. (This multimillion-dollar increase could, by itself, easily justify the cost of a space management team.) Establishment of the space management task force is another demonstration that the university is serious about space management.

*Assume Responsibility to Lead.* Planners must recognize that it takes courage and persistence to deal effectively with the issues of power and inequality. For example, in the university's facility audit program, the space administrator initiated an assessment of site factors, such as lighting, walkways, and handicapped access, and site improvements are now made an integral part of each major building project. As a result, areas of shared interest, such as landscaped pathways, are funded along with particular building projects. In addition to being an advocate of common areas, such as with the university's classrooms and corridor improvement project, the university space administrator initiates programs for those with relatively little political clout where there are known physical deficiencies. Funds for planning major capital renewal improvements have been approved for the music department, and similar projects are being promoted for such departments as Air Force officers training, anthropology, and art. When organizing for space management, it is important for planners both to select personnel with leadership capabilities and to locate them within the organization where initiatives can be effective.

*Be Sensitive to Political Realities.* Being aware of sensitive issues does not preclude planners from stating their position and its rationale. There are institutionally acceptable ways of being proactive. Involving those affected at all levels of decision making is essential, particularly when analyzing sensitive issues and making recommendations. For example, the university's vice-presidential planning group might first be briefed on a situation, request a study, and then review and act on an issue involving more than one vice-president. Similarly, a vice-president might act on a space issue within his or her jurisdiction. The strategy—and it is a critical one—is to have an obvious and acceptable relationship between the chief decision makers and the office of space management.

### Increased Emphasis on Outcomes

Do whatever works—that is increasingly the mode of operation in the nation's institutions of higher education. Survival and practicality have made a results orientation a winning style. Procedures must still be followed, but they are followed as the means to an end, not as the end itself. The increased emphasis on an outcomes-based approach has strengthened the desirability of relating space management to financial operations.

The university's facility audit program has a sound methodology and accepted criteria. However, it is the program's results orientation that makes it effective. Because the emphasis of the program strategies has shifted from process to the identification of legitimate capital renewal projects, increased acceptance has been achieved. By relating physical and functional needs to a clear and seemingly obvious solution—a renewal project—the facilities audit program has become another important tool for the integration of academic, fiscal, and facility objectives.

*Emphasize the Importance of Effective Implementation Strategies.* Understanding that broad acceptance is crucial to effective implementation, the university space administrator has adjusted several procedures and analytical tools. Participation by space coordinators at the department level and support from higher-level administrators have significantly improved the accuracy of the space inventory. For example, replacing the mailed survey with on-site discussions has made updates to the space inventory both more complete and more accurate. Space guidelines that seemed inappropriate were analyzed, and recommendations for change were recommended to top-level decision makers. In one case, an administrative office space guide has been accepted as a reasonable tool for internal analyses and projections. These examples support the space management strategy of employing and supporting personnel who can balance the ideal with the practical, who can balance an understanding of procedures with what really works, and who can bring timely closure to a project for effective implementation.

*Accept That Activities Must Proceed Before Analyses Are Complete.* Intellectually, we know that manageable pieces of the problem must be identified for a near-term solution. However, the need to be comprehensive and the understanding that problems (and their solutions) are usually related seem to complicate matters. Likewise, the effort to be thorough can extend data collection and analysis beyond a time deemed reasonable by others. To avoid analysis paralysis, space managers must define a realistic scope of work and schedule, gain broad acceptance for a particular program, and see a project through to completion. For example, in a recent administrative space realignment analysis conducted by the university's office of space administration, study components were reduced to those considered to be most essential and urgent. The resulting recommendations were transmitted with cost estimates to the executive assistant to the president. The office will follow up on the suggested space changes by facilitating agreement among the vice-presidential units that are affected. The less urgent but perhaps no less important components are now being studied.

## Increased Use of Analysis and Computer-Assisted Information Management

The cost-benefit ratio of automation for space management is improving significantly. Hamer (1988) reports that the percentage of facility management tasks worth automating has changed from about one-third in 1965 to about two-thirds in 1985. Space analysis is probably the task that has most benefited from automation of graphic and nongraphic data bases, and it is therefore an increasingly important and requested space management tool.

As a consequence of this trend, staff need increasing technical sophistication. With the advances in computer technologies and applications, space management personnel with the skills needed for the use of automated systems have had to be hired or developed.

The university's room inventory serves as the basis for determining the area assigned to research and other activities, tracking the acquisition and maintenance of equipment, and scheduling classes and other events. For improved communications and consistency among computer data bases, the University of Virginia has developed programs to relate space, personnel, budget, and equipment files. The indirect costs of space for sponsored programs can now be calculated by comparing researchers, their funding, and their designated space. The accuracy of the people and equipment assigned to a particular room can now be verified. In addition, scaled computer drawings that can be related to nongraphic or tabular information about each room are now being developed. These drawings will aid in verification and improve the overall consistency of the information.

*Promote Analytical Approaches That Are Not Exclusively Quantitative.* The University of Virginia has developed a methodology to balance academic, financial, and facility needs in terms of both function and environmental quality. The facilities audit program analyzes physical conditions and how well academic purposes are satisfied. Academic spaces are periodically analyzed in terms of utilization, and facilities with poor performance are further studied for improvement. Functional concerns, such as accessibility, noise, ventilation, and other qualitative issues, are factored in narrative form with more easily quantified data, and recommendations are made biennially to program and budget decision makers. Space managers must have the ability to understand and communicate both the techniques and methods of science and the values and forms of art if they are to explain and act on such issues as space flexibility, suitability, and utilization.

*Enhance the Planning Effectiveness of Other Managerial Activities.* Providing support for and service to others is the job of space management. When others are helped to become more effective, space managers look more effective. Sometimes creativity is necessary in this collaborative effort. For example, the university registrar had a problem of small classes and large classrooms. The space administrator worked with budget, physical plant, and academic personnel to establish and implement a classroom improvement program whereby large underutilized classrooms were subdivided into more efficient seminar-type rooms.

When organizing for space management, planners must hire and maintain personnel with business, architectural, behavioral science, and academic skills and position them where integration of viewpoints is facilitated.

## Increased Interest in Preserving Older Facilities

College and university buildings are no exception to the national interest in historic preservation. Campuses in higher education contain some of America's best examples of various styles of architecture. Because of image and the relative stability of campuses, community and academic leaders and institutional friends seem to view our campuses as a preserve.

Nostalgic alumni of the University of Virginia want buildings as they experienced them. A large addition in matching historical style was recently built for the University's School of Commerce facility. The addition was made possible in part by a generous contribution from an alumnus. Similarly, a substantial donation has been made for a new arts and sciences building that has been planned in a manner showing respect for its historical context. Old buildings that have become functionally obsolete tend not to be demolished but to be remodeled, often at a cost greater than that required for a new structure. Interior spaces can be gutted, while the exterior façade retains its original character.

*Link Historical Values and Financial Planning with Space Management Strategies.* Good space management strategies help to preserve significant pieces of the past. The university has designated a historic district and linked fund-raising efforts to the district. The result has been very favorable. Public grants and private donations have been received to inventory and preserve buildings. Benefactors have also assisted in the restoration of historic open spaces. The variety of preserved building and landscape features serves not only nostalgic interests but retains a valuable collection for academic studies. Space managers should be selected and supported for their recognition that all institutions have an important historical context and for their ability to assist in the identification and preservation of historical values.

*Consider Perceptions of Previous Space Management Activities.* Looking to the past in institutional space planning requires planners to consider both local conditions and similar issues elsewhere. Precedents—what worked and what failed—should be important to space management decision makers. Strategies that worked or failed for other institutions of higher education should also be examined. While reviewing external precedents, planners should analyze local opportunities for and constraints to improved space utilization. When organizing for space management, planners should select personnel for their broad historical and geographic awareness and for their "institutional memories."

**Increasingly Selective Growth and Retrenchment**

The forecast of enrollments in America's colleges and universities shows wide regional and state variations. Each academic institution must respond to shifts in demographics while not compromising in its areas of strength. In addition, research and teaching institutions are responding to requests from sponsors and constituents for more interdisciplinary studies.

At the University of Virginia, emphasis is being placed on strong programs clustered in geographic zones that maximize the opportunity for shared resources and interdisciplinary studies. A new chemical engineering building will be built for teaching and research as a link between the chemistry department and the school of engineering and applied sciences. Expansion of the science precinct is being planned to include a new building that will combine spaces for a computer science program with those of academic computing services.

The corollary to this trend is the increased need for external funding. The costs of student tuition and fees, which are rising faster than the rate of inflation, are just two indications of the increased need for external funding. Cutbacks in federal programs and the inability of states to make up the resulting differences put more pressure on our nation's colleges and universities to get outside funds.

The University of Virginia's rector has stated that programs that seek increased research support must have the ability both to generate matching funds and to provide adequate space for expansion. As a result, targeted growth in specific instructional units and in areas that can support research through external funding benefit from specific space management strategies, such as the expansion just mentioned of the science precinct.

*Encourage Space Management at All Levels of the Organization.* The strategy of encouraging space management at all levels of the organization is especially important for the trend of increasingly selective growth and retrenchment. While expansion or contraction in programs is a policy issue, decision makers at all levels of an institution benefit from space management information. For example, in response to a need for more administrative space, a recent University of Virginia study identified an opportunity for reduction in staff housing in an area suitable for administration. This opportunity is now understood by top-level decision makers, and several proposals for alternate use of the housing are under consideration.

*Build Flexibility into the Space Management Process.* Just as the building just mentioned is being considered for a change in use, an institution's approach to space management must be adaptable, and the space management team must remain aware of and continuously integrate change. Flexibility in the space management process is essential in remaining responsive and effective. For example, the university's space management policy allocates inventory responsibilities for the health sciences to that department; other units are directly supported by the office of the university space administrator. The flexibility to work with units having an appropriate degree of autonomy while not relinquishing space administration's ultimate responsibility for reporting enhances the opportunity for the space management program to be successful in the long term. Senior-level space managers should be organizationally positioned to enhance flexibility in the decision-making process. At the University of Virginia, the space management function is placed with the vice-president for administration, who oversees related operations, such as administrative computing services, personnel administration, and physical plant planning and support. More informal links are made with academic, financial, and institutional research managers.

**Focus on Upgrading Teaching and Research
Facility Conditions**

College and university buildings are becoming functionally obsolete before they are physically obsolete. As a result, space alterations are becoming both more frequent and larger in area than new construction. The increase in space modifications is being accelerated by rapid changes in technology, especially in areas of research. Simultaneously, research sponsors and academicians are expressing their rising expectations for upgrading and renewing spaces. In response to these needs, institutions are stepping up the frequency and scope of facility and related program evaluations.

The University of Virginia's facility audit program has led to the funding of a major capital renewal project focused on the rehabilitation of Old Cabel Hall. Designed by the New York architect Stanford White and built in 1898, this significant building requires more than $3 million of renewal work without any changes in room configuration or use. The program evaluation component of the building's audit recommended no change in use. The renewal project calls for phased improvements upgrading conditions to current code requirements. The project has been coordinated with other funded projects, such as access for the handicapped. The audit program, like other features of the university's planning process, is ongoing, and it is one of the many important practices that support integration of space management in institutional decision making.

*Integrate Financial, Academic, Physical, and Human Resource Factors in Institutional Planning Periods and Schedules.* Improvements to existing academic spaces must be planned around the school calender. For example, classroom improvements are scheduled for the narrow windows of time between semesters. The office of the university space administrator coordinates furniture or equipment orders and work by various trades, including painting, floor tiling, carpeting, lighting, window treatment, and mechanical. When organizing for space management, planners must keep in mind the functional relationships of project planning, implementation, and control—within institutional time periods.

*Continually Reevaluate Facility Plans and Planning Processes.* Anticipation is the key to effective space management. Periodic review and evaluation of academic, financial, and facility conditions should result in a position of preparedness for space changes. To make their support useful to many decision makers, space managers should project or forecast the most probable courses of action in a time framework. Combined with master site planning efforts that identify recommended uses of various areas, space management is an essential component in the institutional planning process. There is a close relationship between evaluation and anticipated use of academic and related spaces. Consequently, planners must organize for condition surveys, programming of new and remodeled facilities, and master site plan incorporation. A successful space management program requires personnel who have an ability and interest in integrated planning.

## Conclusions

Those interested in organizing for space management should consider current trends and the structure of their institution as well as choose the right people for the job. An awareness of trends, both internal and external, will begin to prepare the institutional planner to recommend the best use of space. Organizationally positioning the space management function to involve decision makers at all levels will support the integration of academic, financial, and facility viewpoints.

To make the most of an appropriate organizational position, space managers should select and develop staff who have skill in conflict resolution to support multiple decision makers, develop useful space inventories and studies, identify suitable criteria and creative solutions, understand quality program issues, and develop capital improvement projects. Ideal staff members use appropriate building evaluation techniques to analyze space utilization standards, clarify responsibilities and initiate desirable plans, provide and implement a timely response, establish planning methods related to the past, and develop an effective space management process. These individuals are team-oriented, open-minded, academically and financially skilled, assertive, technically sophisticated, facility-, action-, and future-oriented facilitators, organizers, and coordinators.

Two primary objectives of a space management unit are to establish and to maintain a current space of inventory that can form a basis for analysis and recommendations. In working to accomplish the purposes of improved space management, the unit must be dedicated to accuracy in data collection for both internal and external reporting, and it must be committed to developing space utilization studies in a timely manner. The staff must be ready to assist in survey responses, capital outlay development, equipment reporting, events and maintenance scheduling, indirect-cost calculations, real estate transactions, and long-range planning.

The diversity of desirable space management characteristics and the variety of space management tasks make planning and organizing essential for success. An effective space management program will be the result of continuing efforts to integrate the function at all levels of decision making. Through anticipation, planning, and organizing, institutions can manage their space as well as their financial and human resources.

## References

Castaldi, B. *Educational Facilities*. Boston: Allyn & Bacon, 1987.

Cavanaugh, R. B. *How to Manage Space*. Winchester, Mass.: R. B. Cavanaugh Publications, 1984.

Hamer, J. M. *Facility Management Systems: Organizing Data for Architectural Programming*. New York: Van Nostrand Reinhold, 1988.

Marsh, D. C., and Griffith, W. J. "Management of the Space Resource: Space Cost Budgeting." *Council of Educational Facility Planners International Journal*, September–October 1985.

*Daniel A. Montgomery is university space administrator at the University of Virginia and a nationally registered architect and certified planner.*

*The Massachusetts Institute of Technology INSITE (INstitutional Space Inventory TEchnique) system is a method developed specifically to provide management information for decision making in the planning stages. A consortium of users applies the system and exchanges information and management techniques.*

# The M.I.T. INSITE
# Space System

## Kreon L. Cyros

Space inventory must be the first step in any space planning and management methodology. There are three critical questions: What do we have? How well are we using it? When do we need more or less? Corporate survival can and often does depend ultimately on the answers to these and related questions. The answers are based on the best information available at the time. The information available can range from little or none to all encompassing; it can vary from qualitative judgment to quantitative fact. Decision makers require accurate and timely data available only from management information systems (MISs). These systems are designed to facilitate the efficient storage, retrieval, and maintenance of large data files. They have been implemented in a number of diverse applications, including facilities management.

Implementing such a system focuses on the structure of the data file, the management of the data file independent of the applications programs that access the data, methods and procedures for updating and changing the data file that preserve its integrity and security, the timeliness with which the data file can be accessed, and location of overall responsibility for administration of the data file. MISs are well suited to applications that require the compilation of lists or reports of data records that meet a set of specific criteria. For example, in the facilities

H. H. Kaiser (ed.). *Planning and Managing Higher Education Facilities.*
New Directions for Institutional Research, no. 61. San Francisco: Jossey-Bass, Spring 1989.

management environment, the maintenance of an organization's room inventory is an excellent facilities management information application. The resulting data base could contain each space's unique identification, such as a room number; a description of its architectural function, area, and organizational assignment; and a myriad of other attributes of the space, such as the moveable equipment residing in it. A typical management report produced from this inventory would list all the buildings whose major architectural functions had changed by more than 5 percent of the total building area in the past twelve months and the details of those specific changes. An ad hoc query of the same data base could provide data concerning the replacement cost of all oscilloscopes more than seven years old in the research divisions.

## The INSITE System

The M.I.T. INSITE (INstitutional Space Inventory TEchniques) system is a management information system developed specifically to provide facilities management information for decision making in the planning stages. INSITE is a data base management system created for the storage, manipulation, analysis, and reporting on vast quantities of M.I.T. facilities data. Since 1973, M.I.T. has shared the INSITE technology with a consortium of users from academic, health care, corporate, and other institutions. Consortium members receive a sophisticated and well-supported computerized management tool and an environment in which facilities management colleagues can exchange information and management techniques. INSITE is designed primarily for facilities managers, planners, and cost accountants. Use of INSITE does not require prior computer training.

In November 1970, the Massachusetts Institute of Technology produced the first space inventory reports from INSITE II, a system designed to address the facilities allocations, operation, and planning issues facing M.I.T. Both the audience and the focus for the INSITE system have changed a great deal since those early days. The audience has grown from a single user to a sizable user's consortium comprising a multitude of facilities management approaches within university, hospital, business, and government environments. INSITE is still used to provide regular reports and special studies for space allocation and facilities planning. However, these recent years have focused increasingly on the system's need to inventory and report on various activities housed within individual spaces. Most recently, INSITE is being used to support the determination of indirect cost recovery rates, an essential cost accounting activity, for facilities users.

The newly designed INSITE 3 system, like the original INSITE system that it replaces, is a space accounting system. It focuses on the inventory of individual rooms, their associated assignment, physical properties, qualities, and quantities as they pertain to a greatly expanded menu of space attributes. Figure 1 shows how the INSITE system organizes facilities space data. The fundamental feature is the basic space record with related attribute records.

When the design of INSITE 3 was being considered, it became apparent from both M.I.T.'s specific needs and from the needs reported by individual consortium members that a room-by-room inventory could be the host for a myriad of other data elements if those elements were viewed as the attributes of an individual space. For example, an equipment inventory could be an integral part of a space inventory if each separable and identifiable piece of equipment was inventoried as individual equipment records associated with the space in which it was located.

**Six Basic INSITE 3 Capabilities**

The INSITE 3 system has been designed to provide its users with six important and very complex capabilities. The first is a data management capability that is both relational in nature and tied to hierarchical files; this unique structure applies specifically to data for facilities management applications. The system provides a special field, called the *space name,* that includes building, floor, and room designations. INSITE is a general data management system fine-tuned to apply specifically to facilities data management needs on IBM or compatible hardware.

Second, INSITE 3 provides a problem-oriented language of English-like commands in a free format. The system is designed to be used by cost accountants, planners, facilities managers, and property administrators, thus avoiding a dependency upon computer programmers or systems engineers by those end users requiring access to the information. Through this technique, the system becomes a tool for the management and planning of space and equipment, not a restrictive crutch.

Third, the system has an extremely powerful report generation capability. There is virtually no mix of data elements within a user's data base that cannot be reported on either in an outline or in a columnar format. The report generator has a myriad of subtotaling and totaling capabilities and final report output selections that range from hard copy to magnetic tape records. Magnetic tape is useful for transferring INSITE data to other information systems within the user's environment.

Fourth, INSITE 3 has been programmed with a full set of algebraic and logical functions providing complete computing capabilities for any quantitative or qualitative data elements available within the data base. These algebraic functions facilitate the development of customized utili-

**Figure 1. INSITE Data Organization**

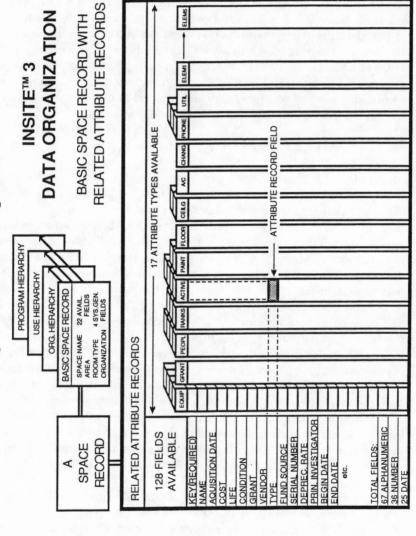

INSITE™ 3
DATA ORGANIZATION

BASIC SPACE RECORD WITH
RELATED ATTRIBUTE RECORDS

M I T OFFICE OF FACILITIES MANAGEMENT SYSTEMS

zation ratios, the measurement of individual space deviations from user-specified norms, and the calculation of straight-line or accelerated depreciation of equipment.

Fifth, the system has a powerful and flexible data selection capability. Users can focus on specific types of data for input, update, and report purposes.

Sixth, although INSITE is a batch processing system, an interactive front-end processor provides a syntax-free screen with full value-checking capability for convenient data entry.

## Data Collection

*Floor Plans.* Any large data collection effort in facilities management requires scaled, reasonably current floor plans. At a minimum, these floor plans must show single-line interior walls, detailed exterior walls, and the locations of columns, doors, and exterior windows. The minimum information required is a unique space name that identifies the room number, floor number, and building number of each space on the plan. Some additional room information can be helpful if it fits within the outline of the room and is legible. In order of usefulness, this information includes architectural function (for example, office, laboratory), organizational assignment (for example, accounting office, engineering department), and area to the nearest square foot or tenth of a square meter.

Floor plans should be drawn in ink on wash-off mylar or, at the very least, in number 2 pencil on linen or a similar medium. Great care should be taken to preserve the originals—for example, by limiting access to them. The first step in getting floor plans when none exist is to get copies of the architect's original plans or, better, yet, a reproducible copy of the design drawings corrected to show what was actually built. In the United States, the most common scale for these drawings is one-fourth inch or one-eighth inch per foot. A very practical scale for working floor plans is one-sixteenth inch per foot, which is approximately one two-hundredth of full scale. Architectural service and supply houses usually have capabilities for photographically reducing or enlarging drawings at other scales.

*Physical Audits.* The best way of gathering the information needed for updating scaled floor plans is to make a physical audit of the space room by room with floor plans in hand. Beginning at the top of a facility (psychologically, it is better to walk down the stairs to begin the audit of a new floor than it is to climb the stairs), each room should be observed quickly. The use of a master key is an obvious must if doors are locked, but always remember to knock first even before inserting the key in the lock. If the facilities auditors can gather the necessary information from a few seconds in the space, questions and complaints from occupants can be almost totally eliminated. If a space does not conform to the floor plan, use the built-in grid system found in most facilities to sketch the partition locations. These grids include such items as internal and external columns, window locations, floor tiles, and ceiling tiles. The auditor needs a large clipboard to hold the plans of the floors to be surveyed, several sharp pencils, a small flashlight for dark spaces, a twelve-foot (or several-meter) retractable metal ribbon tape, and, if possible, a set of master keys. Some visible form of identification, such as a company badge with photograph, and an authorization memo for the audit activity signed by some senior organizational officer are also valuable.

The primary space data to be collected during an audit involve the changes in architectural function and physical configuration. The "old" plans can be brought up to date via the field notes in the comfort of the auditor's office. Each updated space can then be scaled, and its area can be calculated. The area of the nonassignable spaces for circulation and for custodial and mechanical uses should also be scaled. At this point, the audit has produced three of the four pieces of information required for the inventory: the space name or room number for each space, the area, and the architectural function observed by the auditor.

*Departmental Assistance.* The final piece of information required for the minimal space inventory is the organizational assignment of each space—both the nonassignable space (circulation, custodial, and mechanical) and the assignable space (classrooms, laboratories, offices, and so forth). This information is best collected by meeting with the person in the department who knows the most about its facilities. Long-term employees can usually provide a wealth of information when shown up-to-date floor plans. Such persons can be useful contacts for additional data collection efforts in the future. Departmental representatives might appreciate a special report from the data concerning their spaces.

## Data Storage

After the facilities data are collected, the ways in which they are stored and retrieved must be considered. There are three levels of implementation techniques for the storage and retrieval of data elements: the hand posting and manual sorting of data elements, simple computer tabulations of machine-recorded data, and an MIS system, like INSITE, designed specifically for facilities management.

The hand posted room data record technique is quite adequate for meeting the basic inventory requirements of organizations that lack computers and that do not require an automated approach. Organizations whose facilities total less than 250,000 square feet typify this level of implementation. The simplest technique for implementing computer tabulations of facilities inventory data and calculations of space utilization ratio analyses is to convert the hand posted data elements into some machine-readable form. This effort can be accomplished either during the initial data collection phase or, if hand posted records already exist, by converting the existing data.

The management information system approach, which is usually unavoidable for organizations with facilities in the range of 500,000 square feet and beyond, differs from the computer tabulations approach in two ways: the level of technical sophistication that is required and the level of use of the captured data. Organizations that desire to make more effective use of facilities data require more advanced information systems to increase the utility of their data.

Although most managers will define people, dollars, and facilities as the three basic resources available to meet the goals of their organization, few have devoted the same level of energy and expertise in applying computer techniques to their facilities resources as they have to the other two. Many organizations lack either the extensive software development funds or the cadre of systems programmers required for an MIS approach. However, such systems do exist, and consortium arrangements can provide cost-conscious institutions and organizations with access to the system that they need. Such consortium or sharing arrangements enable organizations to make sophisticated use of facilities inventory data, to study space utilization, and to plan for the future of the organization's facilities with no investment in systems development. This implementation strategy can well provide for a broader, more strategic range of institutional planning and management perspectives. The value of sharing information and ideas with colleagues working toward the same goals can be even greater. The overall benefits will far exceed the costs.

**Data Retrieval**

As in any database management system, stored data must be retrieved and arranged in a useful form for the user. Figures 2 and 3 exemplify the most frequently used INSITE space reports at M.I.T. Reports can tabulate information on net usable areas, major users, room classifications, departments and room references, and buildings, including user and room list information. Users can construct reports to suit their needs and specifications. In addition, data from the INSITE system can be retrieved as an ASCII file that can be transferred to other systems, such as accounting and budgeting systems.

**The INSITE-CAD System**

INSITE-CAD, a computer-aided drafting system that operates on an IBM PC/AT or compatible, links to the mainframe INSITE database.

# Figure 2. INSITE Space Inventory Report: Net Usable Area Summary

| | AREA | AREA % OF NUSF | AREA % OF TYPE | SPACES | SPACE % OF TYPE | AVERAGE AREA | AVE AREA INDEX |
|---|---|---|---|---|---|---|---|
| ASSIGNABLE | | | | | | | |
| CLASSROOMS | 190234 | 2.36 | 3.16 | 250 | 1.32 | 761 | 2.39 |
| GENERAL USE | 469633 | 5.81 | 7.80 | 1112 | 5.89 | 422 | 1.32 |
| LABORATORIES | 1224496 | 15.16 | 20.34 | 2881 | 15.25 | 425 | 1.33 |
| OFFICES | 1529954 | 18.94 | 25.41 | 8128 | 43.03 | 188 | 0.59 |
| RESIDENTIAL | 843164 | 10.44 | 14.01 | 3324 | 17.60 | 254 | 0.80 |
| RSCH HEALTH CARE | 39609 | 0.49 | 0.66 | 265 | 1.40 | 149 | 0.47 |
| SPECIAL USE | 265239 | 3.28 | 4.41 | 316 | 1.67 | 839 | 2.63 |
| STUDY | 210704 | 2.61 | 3.50 | 252 | 1.33 | 836 | 2.62 |
| SUPPORT | 1214758 | 15.04 | 20.18 | 2264 | 11.99 | 537 | 1.68 |
| UNCLASSIFIED | 32632 | 0.40 | 0.54 | 95 | 0.50 | 343 | 1.08 |
| TOTAL ASSIGNABLE AREA | 6020423 | 74.53 | 100.00 | 18887 | 100.00 | 319 | 1.00 |
| | | | | | | | |
| NON ASSIGNABLE | | | | | | | |
| CIRCULATION AREA | 1321232 | 16.36 | 64.27 | 4101 | 50.77 | 322 | 1.27 |
| CUSTODIAL AREA | 52244 | 0.65 | 2.54 | 721 | 8.93 | 72 | 0.28 |
| MECHANICAL AREA | 682420 | 8.45 | 33.19 | 3255 | 40.30 | 210 | 0.82 |
| TOTAL NON ASSIGNABLE AREA | 2055896 | 25.46 | 100.00 | 8077 | 100.00 | 255 | 1.00 |
| | | | | | | | |
| TOTAL NET USEABLE AREA | 8076319 | 100.00 | * | 26964 | * | 300 | |

Figure 3. INSITE Space Inventory Report: Department Room List

| | AREA | ROOM TYPE | PAINT DATE | FLOORING | COMMENT |
|---|---|---|---|---|---|
| **BUILDING 9** | | | | | |
| 9 - 306 | 55 | STORAGE FACILITY | 01/67 | | |
| 9 - 307 | 51 | OFFICE SERVICE | 01/67 | | |
| 9 - 308 | 50 | OFFICE SERVICE | 01/67 | | |
| 9 - 312 | 104 | OFFICE SERVICE | 01/67 | WW | |
| 9 - 318 | 11 | OFFICE SERVICE | 01/67 | | |
| 9 - 326 | 112 | OFFICE | 01/67 | WW | |
| 9 - 328 | 100 | OFFICE | 01/67 | WW | |
| 9 - 332 | 159 | OFFICE | 01/67 | WW | |
| 9 - 507 | 51 | KITCHEN FACIL | 01/67 | TILE | |
| 9 - 511 | 106 | OFFICE | 05/76 | RUG | |
| 9 - 513 | 106 | OFFICE | 01/67 | RUG | |
| 9 - 515 | 141 | OFFICE | 03/76 | RUG | |
| 9 - 517 | 158 | OFFICE | 01/67 | RUG | |
| 9 - 519 | 74 | SEC/RECEPTION RM | 01/67 | TILE | |
| 9 - 521 | 108 | OFFICE | 01/67 | RUG | |
| 9 - 523 | 114 | OFFICE | 01/67 | RUG | |
| 9 - 525 | 117 | OFFICE | 01/67 | RUG | |
| 9 - 527 | 105 | OFFICE | 03/76 | RUG | |
| 9 - 529 | 206 | OFFICE | 01/67 | RUG | |
| 9 - 535 | 206 | OFFICE SERVICE | 01/67 | WW | |
| 9 - 537 | 139 | SEC/RECEPTION RM | 01/67 | WW | |
| 9 - 539 | 73 | OFFICE | 01/67 | WW | |
| 9 - 541 | 74 | OFFICE | 01/67 | WW | |
| 9 - 543 | 79 | OFFICE | 01/67 | WW | |
| 9 - 547 | 114 | OFFICE | 01/67 | WW | |
| 9 - 549 | 114 | OFFICE SERVICE | 02/75 | WW | |
| 9 - 549A | 32 | OFFICE | 01/67 | RUG | |
| 9 - 635 | 168 | OFFICE | 01/67 | RUG | |
| 9 - 639 | 77 | OFFICE | 01/67 | RUG | |
| 9 - 641 | 69 | OFFICE | 01/67 | RUG | |
| 9 - 643 | 78 | OFFICE | 01/67 | RUG | |
| BLDG 9 TOTAL | 3151 | | | | |
| **BUILDING 10** | | | | | |
| 10 - 400 | 332 | SEC/RECEPTION RM | 11/72 | WW | |
| 10 - 400A | 16 | OFFICE SERVICE | 11/72 | | |
| 10 - 400B | 16 | OFFICE SERVICE | 11/72 | | |
| 10 - 401 | 440 | CONFERENCE RM | 08/83 | TILE | |
| 10 - 402 | 300 | OFFICE | 01/68 | WW | |
| 10 - 403 | 156 | OFFICE | 01/68 | WW | |
| 10 - 404 | 138 | OFFICE | 01/68 | WW | |
| 10 - 411 | 28 | KITCHEN FACIL | 01/86 | TILE | |
| 10 - 417 | 155 | OFFICE | 01/86 | RUG | |
| 10 - 419 | 181 | OFFICE | 01/86 | RUG | |
| 10 - 419A | 3 | OFFICE SERVICE | 01/86 | | |
| BLDG 10 TOTAL | 1765 | | | | |

TOTAL URBAN ST & PLAN 15799

INSITE-CAD is used to digitize and display scaled floor plans. With INSITE-CAD, drawing changes that affect room number, size, function, or assignment automatically update the INSITE data base and provide a graphic response to data base queries.

INSITE-CAD identifies a room as a unique entity and associates relevant information with the graphic representation. It calculates room areas to either partition centerline or interior wall surfaces. It provides for instant query of floor plan areas, wall dimensions, and thickness. It allows floor plan data to be sent directly to the INSITE data base for updating and thereby eliminates the double handling of facilities data in both CAD and data base files. It accepts instructions from the data base for annotating floor plan displays. For example, an INSITE report that selects rooms meeting certain criteria can be downloaded to the CAD system, which calls forth the appropriate floor plans and crosshatches the rooms selected. Finally, INSITE-CAD links to printers and plotters, offers DXF-formatted output, and is easy to learn and operate.

The hardware environment for INSITE-CAD includes an IBM/AT Model 99 with a math coprocessor chip, a color graphics adaptor and monitor, a high-resolution monitor with color display controller, and a digitizer with sixteen-button cursor. Additional items include extra memory, cables, serial ports, printer, and plotter. Additional enhanced graphic adaptor information stations can be used.

A new capability, CADVIEW, can read drawing files created by INSITE-CAD. It permits space managers, office planners, and departmental administrators, for example, to read but not alter CAD floor plans. All information from floor plans is easy to obtain, and ad hoc queries are easy to conduct. Figure 4 is a response to a query about classroom space on the third floor of the chemical engineering building at M.I.T. The classroom space is represented by the shaded areas. The output facility allows users to construct a picture and output it to a printer or plotter.

## Summary

Precise and timely accounting for physical assets in a college or university is an unavoidable necessity. Physical facilities and capital equipment can represent between 25 and 60 percent of the total assets on an institution's balance sheet. Space and equipment accounting is thus an absolute prerequisite for both management control and fiscal responsibility. The INSITE facilities management information system, developed at M.I.T., provides a tool for addressing these issues in a systematic and precise manner. The recent marriage of the microcomputer-based graphic data file of floor plans provided by INSITE-CAD to the comprehensive mainframe INSITE data base provides an advanced facilities decision

# Figure 4. INSITE CADVIEW Plot:
## Classroom Space, Third Floor, Chemical Engineering Building, M.I.T.

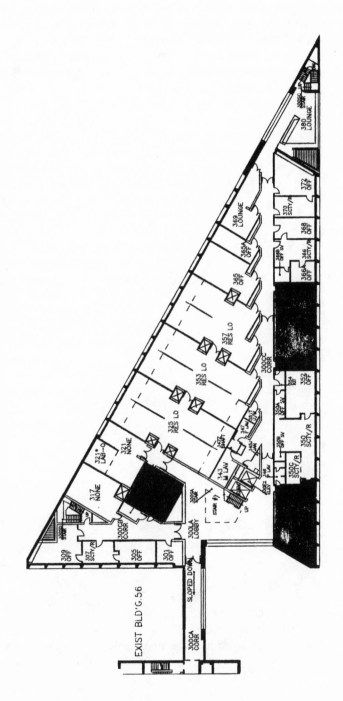

support system. M.I.T.'s Office of Facilities Management System is sharing both the INSITE technology and the expertise needed to implement it effectively with domestic and foreign institutions and corporations preparing for the 1990s. Further information on INSITE can be obtained from the Office of Facilities Management Systems, Massachusetts Institute of Technology, 77 Massachusetts Avenue, Cambridge, Massachusetts 02139.

*Kreon L. Cyros is director of the M.I.T. Office of Facilities Management Systems. From 1966 to 1970 he pioneered the development of computer-aided facilities management software by designing and implementing the INSITE management information system for M.I.T.*

*While space planning guidelines have been in use since the early 1950s, they have recently become more than just a planning tool.*

# Space Planning Guidelines

## Jack Probasco

Space planning guidelines or standards have been in use since the early 1950s. Tremendous demands were placed on colleges and universities after World War II and the Korean War to provide facilities sufficient to handle the influx of students. Administrators realized that they could not continue to assign space haphazardly without using some method for measuring need. Thus, procedures were developed that defined, analyzed, and projected space requirements.

Institutions began to measure and organize data based on the facilities currently in use. Inventories of space characteristics and utilization evolved eventually into space planning guidelines. However, because many of the early guidelines were based on averages of current space, they were unsatisfactory for estimating actual teaching and research space requirements. Measurements based not on existing averages but on a particular demand were needed to gauge the amount of facilities that should be built or remodeled.

It was crucial for the space provided for expanded needs to be adequate because of the lengthy time needed to redesign, construct, and occupy a new building.

The need to plan facilities properly continues today. While demand for the construction of large quantities of various facilities has diminished, the need for forecasting the right amount of space for both new and remodeled facilities continues to be a challenge.

H. H. Kaiser (ed.). *Planning and Managing Higher Education Facilities.*
New Directions for Institutional Research, no. 61. San Francisco: Jossey-Bass, Spring 1989.

It is necessary to update space guidelines continually. Changing technology requires modification of existing space planning guidelines to reflect the space needed to teach and conduct research. For example, the computers used for instruction, research, and administration have placed a demand for more space on the institutions. Faculty and staff offices now require a microcomputer, which increases the amount of space required in each office by approximately fifteen square feet. Classrooms housing computers for each student nearly double the space required for each student station. Institutions using thirteen to seventeen square feet per classroom station in the past now require twenty-five to thirty square feet per station. Universities that have research and public service as part of their mission require additional facilities because of the increasing emphasis on research and cooperative arrangements with private industry. Massive scientific projects now demand the superlative prefix: supercomputing, supertelescopes, superconducting, and supercolliders.

Today's sophisticated laboratories require different amounts of space and different types of space from the laboratories of ten or fifteen years ago. Some modern research laboratories have become very instrument oriented, and equipment occupies considerable space. The biological sciences, chemistry, and other disciplines require specialized space, such as instrumentation laboratories.

Other disciplines have used simulators and computers to miniaturize their research. Space planning guidelines must keep pace with reality and adapt to the changing physical requirements. This chapter discusses some current concepts in estimating space needs.

**Function of Space Planning Guidelines**

Space planning guidelines serve primarily as a planning tool. They are also used to document proposals to state coordinating or governing boards and state legislatures that request additional facilities. A frequent use of guidelines is to assist in institutional decision making. If funds are limited, space planning guidelines can assist in determining resource priorities and costs. An institution can determine how best to use limited funds by comparing individual college or department needs. With so many institutions now considering charging each department or unit for the space that it uses, space planning guidelines can be used as a basis for this as well.

**Need for Updating Space Planning Guidelines**

While higher education space planning guidelines have been in existence for over thirty-five years, they are constantly changing. There are many different types of space planning guidelines depending on the creator's intentions and on what can be accomplished with the available data.

Guidelines are not standards that can be pulled off the shelf and used by every university. Space guidelines for one university may not be useful for another university without some modification. They must be modified to meet the needs of the organization and its methods of teaching and doing research. Therefore, space planning guidelines will vary from institution to institution. They will also vary from year to year if changes are made within an institution.

The reasonableness of any given formula depends on the user's perspective. A formula used to determine the space components of a brand-new community college or university developed during the enrollment explosion of the 1970s might seem reasonable until the new institution's administration tries to fit a changing program mix into its fixed campus of bricks and mortar. The list of additional sources that ends this chapter illustrates the diversity of the guidelines that have been developed over the years.

## Terminology

This chapter describes several approaches and methods for calculating space needs. Following are some commonly used terms in space planning guidelines:

*Assignable square feet* (ASF) refers to all assignable space, excluding mechanical facilities, restrooms, circulation, structure, and other such nonassignable space.

*Weekly student contact hour* (WSCH) refers to the number of hours per week during which students use a facility. For example, a class of thirty students that meets Monday, Wednesday, and Friday from 1:00 to 3:00 P.M. generates 180 WSCHs (30 × 3 × 2). Normally, the time period used for determining the total is from 8:00 A.M. to 5:00 P.M., but it can vary depending on how one uses the guidelines.

*Room utilization rate* is the proportion of actual use to available hours during the average week. For an 8 A.M. to 5 P.M. time period, forty-five hours are available. A room expected to be used thirty hours per week has a 67 percent room utilization rate.

*Station occupancy rate* is the proportion of actual use of each station to available stations when a room is in use. The *station (module) size* is the area devoted to each individual station. Normally, this figure includes the service areas associated with the room that contains the station. For example, a classroom station size of sixteen square feet includes the circulation area, closets, or storage areas within the room. This figure is not a design criterion but rather a number that can be used in conjunction with other parts of the formula to determine the amount of space needed.

*Space factor* is the square foot area that is applied to the demand criteria to determine the size of the area required for a function.

## Applications of Space Planning Guidelines

*Classrooms.* Most guidelines for classrooms are based on the same elements. The amount of classroom space is determined by multiplying the expected weekly student contact hours by the space factor. The space factor is the square foot area that is applied to the demand criteria to determine the size of the area required for a function. For example, the space factor for a doctorate-granting university that offers most of its courses between 8:00 A.M. to 5:00 P.M. Monday through Friday is

$$\frac{15 \text{ square feet}}{(45 \text{ hours} \times .667) \times .625} = .800$$

The space factor (.800) is then multiplied by the weekly student contact hours (the demand criteria) to determine the amount of classroom space required.

The space factor is determined by dividing the assignable square feet (ASF) per student station or station size, by a figure calculated by multiplying the total hours per week during which the room is available for use by the expected room utilization rate and by the expected station occupancy rate when the room is in use. The normal ranges for these elements are:

| | |
|---|---|
| Station size | 11 to 20 square feet |
| Hours | 40 to 74 hours |
| Room utilization rate | 60 to 78 percent |
| Station occupancy rate | 62 to 70 percent |

The selected space factor varies as a function of type of room (classroom, seminar room, lecture hall), type of institution (two-year institution, comprehensive college, doctorate-granting university), length of instructional day (8:00 A.M. to 5:00 P.M., 8:00 A.M. to 10:00 P.M.) and length of instructional week (some institutions include a Saturday half-day for instruction), expected room use, and expected station occupancy rate within rooms in use.

Institutions that do not have utilization data can convert credit hours into contact hours by multiplying the total credit hours for the course or for the college by 1.06. This factor will vary slightly depending on the disciplines offered. For the humanities, the amount of contact hours is nearly the same as the number of credit hours. For the sciences, there are

10 to 15 percent more contact hours than credit hours. The formula just stated yields the total amount of contact hours for all types of rooms in use. To determine the contact hours for classrooms only, multiply the figure by 75 percent. This percent varies by discipline. For example, lab-intensive courses, such as biological sciences and the arts, have a smaller percentage of their courses in classrooms.

*Teaching Laboratories.* The space calculation for teaching laboratories rooms is similar to the space calculation for classrooms. However, the percent of classroom use as compared to other types of rooms will vary by discipline. Teaching laboratory space needs are calculated by applying a station module size to a use factor (combination of room use and station occupancy goals) and to the department's or discipline's total weekly contact hours in teaching labs. For example, 75 square feet per station × .056 use factor × 2,000 WSCHs = 8,400 square feet. Most guidelines in use across the country use a room use rate of 45 to 55 percent, with the majority at the lower end of the range.

For some departments, this use factor of 50 percent may be hard to achieve. For example, certain engineering departments (including ceramic, electrical, and mechanical) may need several specialized laboratories rather than one or two similarly constructed labs (such as in chemistry). The use factor for these specialized laboratories may be as low as 33 percent or fifteen hours per week.

On rare occasions, the use factor may be acceptable at 25 percent or 11.25 hours per week, since the laboratories are necessary for instruction in that particular subject, even if they have very limited use. The department of Theatre is an example. Such departments as Architecture, Art, and Photography have considerable amounts of individual study within the teaching laboratories or studios. It is assumed that these labs are used 65 percent of the time or approximately 45 hours per week, based on a room availability of seventy hours 8:00 A.M. to 10:00 P.M. The assumption is that approximately one-third of the time (fifteen hours) is used for individual study, and the remaining two-thirds (thirty hours) is used for instruction.

The occupancy rate of work stations within occupied labs ranges between 70 and 85 percent, with 80 percent being average.

The normal use factor (combination of room use rate and station occupancy rate) is .056. The formula from which this value is developed is as follows:

$$\frac{1}{(50 \text{ percent of } 45 \text{ hours})} \times \frac{1}{.80} = .056$$

For departments that need many different specially equipped labs, such as welding engineering, the formula is the following:

$$\frac{1}{(33 \text{ percent of } 45 \text{ hours})} \times \frac{1}{.80} = .083$$

For departments, such as architecture, in which a large amount of individual study takes place in the labs during both day and evening, the formula is:

$$\frac{1}{(65 \text{ percent of } 70 \text{ hours})} \times \frac{1}{.90} = .024$$

And, for departments, such as art, in which a large amount of individual study takes place during the day hours, the formula is:

$$\frac{1}{(60 \text{ percent of } 45 \text{ hours})} \times \frac{1}{.80} = .046$$

While teaching-lab station sizes vary by discipline, they can also vary by institution. For example, the module or station size may vary accordingly.

| | |
|---|---|
| Architecture | 55 to 80 square feet |
| Electrical engineering | 80 to 100 square feet |
| Industrial and management engineering | 70 to 120 square feet |
| Physical sciences | 60 to 75 square feet |
| Social sciences | 30 to 50 square feet |

*Research Laboratories.* The greatest variance in guidelines used by institutions is how space is calculated for research labs. Today's sophisticated laboratories require different amounts and types of space than the laboratories of ten or fifteen years ago. Some modern research laboratories have become very instrument oriented, and equipment occupies considerable space. The biological sciences, chemistry, and other disciplines require special equipment.

Numerous methods are now used for determining the amount of research lab space required by each discipline. However, there is consensus as to the formula that should be used for calculating research space:

Number of researchers × the lab module = research lab space

The main difference between the various formulas is in the method of determining the number of researchers. Some universities count each doctoral student and faculty member in doctoral programs as one unit and each master's degree student and faculty member in programs that offer the master's degree as one-half unit. The Ohio State University model uses a varying percentage for each category of user (graduate students, postdoctoral students, faculty members, other researchers) to determine the number engaged in research. The accuracy of this approach requires a good data base. The different percentage of faculty members and graduate students who are doing research at any one time must be known. The figure varies by type of researcher and by discipline.

In determining the station, or module, size, some institutions categorize the laboratory type into groups and allocate the same number of square feet for every department or program in the group. They may categorize the departments into three or four groups. The more equipment-oriented types may require 400 to 500 square feet per researcher, while the other groups may require 250, 100, or 50 square feet per researcher. Other institutions use a different square footage figure for each discipline. The ranges in station size, or lab modules, for various disciplines are as follows:

| | |
|---|---|
| Biological sciences | 275 to 350 square feet |
| Business and management | 60 to 80 square feet |
| Engineering | 250 to 450 square feet |
| Physical sciences | 250 to 375 square feet |
| Psychology | 175 to 225 square feet |
| Social sciences | 75 to 100 square feet |

*Offices.* The total amount of office space required is determined by multiplying the office module by the total number of personnel requiring offices. The office size varies by rank. In most cases, the head count is used for determining the number of personnel requiring offices. If there is a large number of persons with a full-time-equivalency (FTE) of 50 percent or less, the advisability of counting all persons with an FTE of less than 50 percent as FTE rather than as a head count should be considered.

*Faculty.* Since faculty office space is already in place at most universities and since modifying the space to meet some guideline would require extensive remodeling, it is recommended that the current average size for each department be used to calculate its office size, with the following exception. Offices larger than 200 square feet (except for certain disciplines, such as art and music) and offices smaller than 90 square feet are excluded from this average.

A 135-square-foot office is used for departments with an average of lower than that amount, since 135 square feet is the minimal average size. Faculty within certain departments may require offices larger than the 135-square-foot guideline in order to properly conduct their teaching and research activities. Architecture may require 160 square feet; art and music may require even larger ones—250 square feet and 210 square feet, respectively—to accommodate the necessary equipment or musical instruments. They may have little or no need for additional laboratory space, since their offices are classified as office labs.

Here are some typical figures for administrative offices:

| | |
|---|---|
| President | 600 square feet |
| Vice-president, provost | 400 square feet |
| Dean | 350 square feet |
| Chairperson | 240 square feet |
| Assistant vice-presidents, assistant provosts, and assistant deans | 225 square feet |
| Other administrators and professionals | 150 square feet |

*Graduate Students.* Offices are provided for all graduate students who have an appointment of 25 percent FTE or more. The FTE count is used for all graduate students with appointments that total less than 25 percent. Sixty square feet of office space are provided for all graduate teaching assistants, all graduate administrative assistants, and all graduate research assistants who require an office rather than research lab space to perform their work. These offices are normally grouped together to form rooms of 120 or more square feet.

*Clerical Staff.* One hundred square feet of office space are recommended for each staff person. This figure excludes office service space (files, reception area, copy machines) and space for student workers. An additional fifty square feet of space should be provided for each FTE student worker.

*Office Service Space.* While some guidelines now in use calculate office service space and clerical staff space as part of the faculty office calculation, a separate calculation provides a more accurate estimate of the space required. It is suggested that the office service space (space for files, reception area, copy machines, and similar functions) be based on a percentage of the total office space required for a department or college. For departments with less than 15,000 square feet of office space, use 15 percent. For departments with 15,000 to 24,999 square feet of office space, use 13.75 percent. For departments with 25,000 to 34,999 square feet of office space, use 12.5 percent. For departments with 35,000 to 44,999 square feet of office space, use 11.25 percent. For departments with 45,000 or more square feet of office space, use 10 percent, and for college offices and major administrative units, use 20 percent.

*Conference and Lounge Space.* Many guidelines do not address conference and lounge space as a separate item. The amount of space required for the conference and lounge functions is based on the size of the unit, and it should be estimated by a separate calculation. At a minimum, conference and lounge space should be based on twenty square feet per faculty member and professional staff person. For departmental calculations, fifteen square feet is used per person, the remaining five square feet is combined with the college office calculation in order to provide multiuse conference rooms. The same calculation applies to nonacademic units. Each office unit has fifteen square feet per user, while the major administrative unit, such as a vice-president, uses the remaining five square feet.

*Library.* The amount of library space required is determined by adding the following components: reading space, stack space, service space, audiovisual and electronic media facilities, and lounge space and merchandising facilities. Reading space is the product of number of faculty and students times the percent using library facilities times the assignable square feet per reading station. The reading station area varies with the type of station used (carrel, table and chairs, lounge chairs). Normally, thirty square feet per station can be used. To determine the stack space, convert all library documents to a volume count, and multiply the number of volumes by a square-foot-per-volume rate. Service space is a percentage of the total space calculated for the reading space and the stack space. The normal figure is 20 to 25 percent for main libraries and 10 to 15 percent for local or departmental libraries (if binding and other such services are done elsewhere). Base the estimate for audio-visual and electronic facilities on 25 ASF per station. Five percent of the total users will require this type of space at any one time. The figure for lounge space and merchandising facilities can be computed by using an assignable square foot figure per number of library users. Normally, a figure of two to three square feet per user is added to the calculation to allow for some lounge study facilities where food and drink machines are permitted within the library.

*Reading Space.* The most difficult calculation in formulating library space needs lies in determining the number of required reading stations. This determination is especially difficult at large universities that have decentralized libraries. Crossover among users can be high, particularly among undergraduate students from one department or college who use the libraries of other disciplines for study areas. Institutions can relieve this demand by providing additional study areas throughout the campus.

The following figures can be used as a basis for determining the number of reading stations required as a percentage of student and faculty head count: In universities with college and department libraries, the main library requires stations for 10 percent of the lower-division students, 5 percent of the upper-division students, 5 percent of the master's degree students, 5 percent of the doctoral students, and 5 percent of the faculty. The local libraries require stations for 5 percent of the lower-division students, 10 percent of the upper-division students, 20 percent of the master's degree students, 20 percent of the doctoral students, and 5 percent of the faculty. Institutions that do not have local libraries require stations for 15 percent of both the lower-division students and upper-division students, 20 percent of both the master's degree students and doctoral students, and 10 percent of the faculty.

Law libraries have a higher use rate than others. The Association of American Law Schools recommends that 65 percent be used. However, use rates as low as 40 percent are common.

*Stack Space.* The guidelines used for determining stack space are generally standard throughout the country, although there are minor variations in certain assumptions. Assume sixty-six inches (five and a half feet) for two stacks with an aisle of thirty-six inches. Each stack is twelve inches deep. Assume an aisle after every seven stacks (add 15 percent) and an aisle corridor after every tenth row of stacks (add 10 percent). Stacks are seven shelves high. Assume seven volumes per lineal foot and assume stack space to be 70 percent full.

The formula for determining stack space per volume is:

$$\frac{\text{area (square feet)} \times 1.265}{\text{number of stacks} \times \text{number of volumes per stack} \times \text{percent full}}$$

$$\frac{(1 \text{ foot} \times 5 \text{ feet} \times 1.265)}{2 \times (7 \times 7) \times .70} = .092 \text{ square feet per volume}$$

The formula should be adjusted to conform to the needs of each library. For example, book volumes in law libraries are normally larger; therefore, the square foot per volume factor may be .12 to .15 rather than .092.

*Physical Education and Recreation Facilities.* The facilities provided for physical education and recreation vary from one institution to another. Some institutions put a heavy emphasis on physical education and recreational activities, even to the point of making physical education courses mandatory. Others, particularly if land is at a premium, have less concern for providing such space.

While the guidelines in use by various state higher education agencies vary, the following criteria appear to be in common use: A range of twenty to thirty square feet per student is used for the first 1,000 to 1,500 students. After the basic 25,000 to 35,000 square feet, additional space is provided at five to ten square feet per student. While this calculation provides an overall estimate of the total space required, the actual breakdown by type of facility depends on the specific programs at each institution. However, some guidelines on the reasonable amounts of space required for various types of facilities can be stated. These amounts will vary, depending on whether physical education is mandatory or voluntary, on the number of sports clubs, on the number of students engaged in intramural sports, and on the presence of activities that put a demand on the use of facilities. For indoor basketball courts, colleges with mandatory physical education should count on one court per 2,000 students, while colleges with voluntary physical education can count on one court per 3,000 students. One swimming pool is required per 8,000 students.

*Student Computer Areas.* The amount of space required for computer areas within departments that are used for unscheduled computer labs is determined by calculating the computer workstation area requirements and combining them with the space necessary to house any mainframe and peripheral equipment that are required within an office or department. In all cases, colleges and departments start with a base of 100 square feet and add the workstation calculation.

The space required for these workstations is determined by the number of contact hours per FTE student. The number of FTE students is determined by dividing the number of undergraduate credit hours by fifteen and the number of graduate credit hours by twelve. The number of contact hours varies by academic discipline and student level. For the purposes of the present calculation, the *A* group includes art, biological sciences, dentistry, drama and dance, general education, home economics, humanities, journalism, law, military science, music, nursing, optometry, physical education, social work, and veterinary medicine. The *B* group includes agriculture, allied medical, architecture, education, medicine, pharmacy, public administration, and social and behavioral sciences. The *C* group includes business adminstration, mathematics, and physical sciences. The *D* group includes computer science and engineering. The following assumptions can be made about contact hours for discipline groups and student levels:

| Discipline Group | Undergraduate | Graduate |
|---|---|---|
| A | 1-2 | 2-3 |
| B | 2-3 | 3-5 |
| C | 3-6 | 5-7 |
| D | 6-9 | 7-12 |

The amount of space required for each discipline can be calculated by multiplying the assignable square feet space factor by the total number of WSCHs.

The space factor varies with the length of time during which the facilities are available for use and the average occupancy rate when the facilities are in use. The following rates are used within the space factor:

|  | Space Factor (ASF per Workstation) | Hours in Use | Average Occupancy Rate |
|---|---|---|---|
| 8:00 a.m.-10:00 p.m. | 25-35 | 70 per week | 70 percent |
| 8:00 a.m.- 5:00 p.m. | 25-35 | 45 per week | 82.5 percent |

The space factor is determined by multiplying the workstation size by the reciprocal of the hours in use and the reciprocal of the workstation occupancy rate. For example:

$$30 \times \frac{1}{70} \times \frac{1}{.70} = .612$$

$$30 \times \frac{1}{45} \times \frac{1}{.825} = .808$$

The space factor is multiplied by the student contact hours to determine the amount of space required. For example, if there are 1,200 FTE undergraduate students and 100 FTE graduate students in mathematics, the amount of space required is approximately 3,305 square feet:

$$(1,200 \times 4 \times .612) + (100 \times 6 \times .612) = 3,305$$

This calculation provides four rooms with twenty-eight terminals in each. Each terminal requires at least thirty square feet.

Because the data processing facilities used for administrative support functions and other noninstructional purposes are considered office service space within the office area computation, they are excluded from the present calculation. The computer facilities classified as teaching labs because they are used for scheduled computer labs are included in the laboratory calculations. The computer facilities used for research are included under research laboratories. If a space classified as computer facilities is used for both teaching and individual student use, the WSCHs used for teaching must be added to this calculation in determining the total space required.

*Other Assignable Space.* The space needs for other facilities are often determined by observations and discussions with the departments and colleges.

## Conclusion

Many different models for estimating and projecting higher education space requirements are now in use. The references listed in the next section provide examples of standards and methods of application. The guidelines that a particular institution selects depends on its organization, the availability of the data that the models call for, and the amount of work that one wants to do. If an institution has limited information on room usage, inventory, and staffing and faculty counts, it is limited in making realistic projections of space needs.

## Additional Sources

Bareither, H. D., and Schillinger, J. L. *University Space Planning: Translating the Educational Program of a University into Physical Facility Requirements.* Chicago: University of Illinois Press, 1968.

*Educational Facilities: Rules of Florida State Board of Education.* Florida Administrative Code, Chapter 6A-2, 1986.

*Fixed Assets Planning Guidelines and Special Requirements for Institutions of Higher Education.* Virginia State Council of Higher Education, October 7, 1980.

*Law Library Journal* (American Association of Law Libraries), 1987, *79* (3), (entire issue).

Matsler, F. G. *Space and Utilization Standards.* Report to the Coordinating Council for Higher Education. Sacramento, Calif.: California Public Higher Education, September 1966.

Metcalf, K. D. (ed.). *Planning Academic and Research Library Buildings.* Chicago: American Library Association, 1986.

Probasco, J., with the Two-Year Space Planning Advisory Committee. *Space Planning Guidelines for the Public Two-Year Campuses.* Ohio Board of Regents, May 1974.

Probasco, J., with the University Space Planning Advisory Committee. *Space Planning Guidelines for the Public Universities in Ohio.* Ohio Board of Regents, May 1974.

Russell, J. D., and Doi, J. I. *Manual for Studies of Space Utilization in Colleges and Universities.* Athens: American Association of Collegiate Registrars and Admissions Officers, Ohio University, 1957.

*Space Planning Guidelines.* College Park: Office of Facilities Planning, University of Maryland, May 1982.

*Space Planning Guidelines.* Council of Educational Facility Planners, International, July 1985.

*Space Use, Space Needs: The Availability and Use of Public Sector Higher Education Facilities in Texas.* Austin: Coordinating Board, Texas College and University System, April 1980.

*Time and Territory: A Preliminary Exploration of Space and Utilization Guidelines in Engineering and the Natural Sciences.* Sacramento: California Postsecondary Education Commission, February 1986.

*Jack Probasco is facilities planner for the Ohio State University. He has served as a member of the board of directors for the Council of Educational Facility Planners, International.*

*Space standards developed for system-wide application at
a macro level to a broad range of institutions are inadequate
for use in planning at a micro level. What is required is a
responsive, objective process of space analysis that is both
site specific and tailored to individualized departmental use
sufficiently standardized to be not only a consistent but also
an equitable approach to different types of facilities planning.*

# Using Macro Standards
# at a Micro Level:
# Bridging the Gap

Gail Milgrom, Elizabeth Sisam

The past few years have seen a renewed interest in the use of university
space standards and entitlement formulas. Standards developed more than
two decades ago by provincial, state, and federal agencies for system-wide
application at a macro level are currently under scrutiny. During the
period when enrollment in postsecondary institutions was growing at a
significant rate, space standards were used for determining the overall
spatial requirements of institutions within a system. Today, with fewer
iniiiatives in new construction, space standards are being applied in the
redevelopment of existing facilities to meet the demands of new programs
and technologies. Funding agencies responsible for accountability in capital expenditure are increasingly concerned that space standards accurately
define the specific space needs of an institution. The demand for space

---

This chapter is an adaptation of an article published under the title "Bridg-
ing the Gap Between Space Standards and Space Allocation: A Methodology" in
the *Journal of the Society for College and University Planning, Planning for Higher
Education.*

H. H. Kaiser (ed.). *Planning and Managing Higher Education Facilities.*
New Directions for Institutional Research, no. 61. San Francisco: Jossey-Bass, Spring 1989.

standards that can provide a valid basis for decision making is driving this new critical attention.

The redevelopment of space standards and formulas focuses on the distinctive characteristics that make them useful for comparing institutions within a system at a macro level and for reviewing campus space utilization and entitlement:

- Data, or input measures, defined in terms that are common to all institutions that use the standards
- Space factors based not on specific architectural models but on the average sizes of facilities throughout a large jurisdiction
- Generalized assumptions on utilization that cover the wide scope of academic and nonacademic activities within a group of institutions whose members may vary considerably in size and mission.

However, these system-wide space standards and formulas are not as effective when they are used to determine the specific requirements of an individual department in its preparation for new construction, renovation of existing space, or reallocation of facilities. The averages and general assumptions that make the space formulas useful in broad analytical exercises often preclude the sensitivity and comprehensiveness necessary in the development of realistic local space programs.

Incompatibilities become apparent when a space planning document inappropriately matches the input measures and space factors of a set of macro standards to the staff, students, functions, and activities of a particular department. The reasons for the incompatibilities are varied, ranging from differing academic program emphasis to the presence or absence of institutional utilization standards and the limitations of existing structures. The result is often frustration and confusion on the part of planners and users. The recommendations and decisions that have to be made will then rely more on subjective reasoning, expediency, and political strength than on objective criteria.

Another potential area of difficulty is the involvement of the many different levels of administration within an institution that have some responsibility for space planning decisions and allocations. People from a variety of administrative and academic positions whose concerns are quite dissimilar are often placed in the position of being space experts. These administrators must rely on the existing space standards, formulas, policies, and procedures for guidance. Use of a space analysis process and a set of standards that are not sufficiently relevant to diverse situations and accessible to a wide range of people will hamper the progress of planning activities.

The most difficult spatial decisions are those concerning the reallocation of existing departmental space to allow for new and changing activities. These are the decisions that most often have to be made. Reallocation involves identifying underutilized space. The perception that space is being taken away will often offend territorial sensitivities. Standards that are perceived as unrealistic or irrelevant exacerbate the situation.

The space analysis process described in this chapter was designed by facilities planners at the University of Toronto to address the gap between macro standards and the way they are used at the micro level. The process takes a new look at the current macro space standards and presents ways of modifying the most appropriate elements within them for use at a micro planning level. These new customized standards are only one part of the process, which also includes institutional space policies and guidelines, an augmented space inventory, and a well-developed procedure for collecting space utilization data from users. The goal is to create planning tools that will be more sensitive to the internal requirements of the institution than the existing provincial space standards.

## Developing a Space Analysis Process

The recognition that system standards and formulas could not stand on their own when determinations of individual departmental space programs had to be made followed from a series of frustrating attempts to use them in specific planning exercises. Although the space formulas could be calculated, the results were confusing in most instances. The uniqueness of a department, its academic program, the buildings in which it was accommodated, and the existing political environment created a gap that the generalizations and averages inherent in some portions of the space formula could not bridge. Although the results were based on rational and logical standards, they required interpretation, qualification, and explanation. These requirements led to delays and miscommunication between institutional departments.

To address these problems at the University of Toronto, the Office of the Assistant Vice-President, Planning initiated a project to study and develop institutional space standards. The project was carried out in conjunction with the Office of Space Management, which is responsible for the university's space inventory and which reports to the assistant vice-president, planning. The study resulted in the development of a process of space analysis in which customized standards were just one component. This process of space analysis, which was tested within the framework of ongoing planning projects within the university, is now in routine use.

In developing a space analysis process that incorporated space standards sensitive to the unique needs of a particular department or site and that could be used in a consistent and equitable way throughout the institution, four areas requiring attention were identified.

*Customizing the Existing Macro Space Standards.* The first step was a comprehensive evaluation, refinement, and adaptation of the existing provincial space standards—the Council of Ontario Universities' (COU)

(1972, 1978, 1988) *Building Blocks.* The institution was using (and continues to use) the provincial space standards and formulas for reporting on a regular basis to various governmental bodies and as an occasional in-house planning tool for general analysis. However, since the goal of the project was the creation of a set of standards that could be applied equitably and realistically to each sector within the university, the components that shaped the system standard in each of the space categories had to be examined. In some space categories, the individual components of the formula could be broken down and used as is. For example, in scheduled instructional space, the area per station, room utilization, and seat occupancy ratios, once adjusted to reflect institutional conditions, were excellent tools for determining requirements. In other space categories, the usefulness of the individual components was limited, and entirely new approaches had to be developed.

The focus was on the five space categories that are commonly found under the jurisdiction of an academic department: classrooms, teaching laboratories, research laboratories, offices, and general departmental space. Within each of these five categories, the formula, its input measure and space factor (area per station and utilization standard), and the assumptions on which they were based were carefully reviewed and evaluated.

The input measure that drives the need for a particular type of space is the number of full-time-equivalent (FTE) students, equivalent volumes, academic staff, nonacademic staff, graduate students, lab contact hours, and so forth. It was important to understand the system definition of each input measure. It was necessary to have a clear understanding of what was included and what was excluded in order to interpret the results of formula calculations and to deal with the complexities involved in collecting the data. It was found that these input measures, which had good general definitions for collecting information from a broad range of institutions, were not necessarily a true indicator of the number, size, or type of rooms required at the institution itself. For example, the COU formula uses number of FTE students to determine entitlement to classroom facilities. The total space generated by this input measure was not a useful guide for determining the facilities that would be needed to correct existing inefficiencies. A match of section size to classroom capacities and an accounting of timetable restrictions produced a much better result. The new institutional micro standards modified the input measures of the macro standards to make them more accurately reflect the drivers of space need within the institution's own departments. In addition, the input measures became important as the key link between academic program planning and space planning for future activities.

The space factor has two components: the area required for an activity and a utilization standard. The project conducted a review of the bases of the space factors, the assumptions that had shaped them, and current institutional practices in order to determine their appropriateness for the institution's facilities, programs, and policies.

In the provincial space standards, the area required in a particular space category is generally an average of conditions existing at the institutions surveyed when the system standard was developed; it is not representative of a particular room design and layout. This approach worked well for comparisons at the macro level because it allowed for variations between institutions. For departmental or project analysis at the micro level, the area component did not always work as a good guideline. A standard for new construction where sizes could be controlled was not relevant when existing space was being reallocated. For example, the COU standard for faculty offices is 140 square feet, 10 square feet of which is part of the pool for larger-than-standard offices, such as the dean's office. However, a reallocation project in a building in which the average office size was 155 square feet needed to have the 15 square feet variation from standard acknowledged in order to avoid distortion of the space program. In this situation, the number of offices was more important than the total area required. Furthermore, it was found that, in both the instructional and research laboratory categories, the implied area per station was too generalized to recognize variations not only between but within departments. Realistic areas per station were developed, as were guidelines for their application.

A utilization standard provides a yardstick that can measure efficiency of use. Within the provincial space standards, the utilization measures are based on general assumptions about both the probability of use and the institutional policies regarding use: That is, an effectively used classroom is occupied 67 percent of a forty-five-hour week, a standard bookshelf can hold 125 equivalent volumes, every graduate student should have an office-type workstation, an FTE student spends sixteen hours a week in scheduled classroom-type facilities, and so on. The evaluation process revealed that not only did the University of Toronto not conform to these implicit assumptions but that there were significant variations between departments. Attempts to adhere strictly to utilization standards would theoretically result in underhousing for some departments and in overhousing for others. Therefore, each utilization assumption was carefully reviewed for its applicability at institutional and departmental levels.

Institutional space policies and guidelines were developed parallel to these customized space standards so that they could be built into the process. In addition, the analysis phase made an allowance for flexibility so that some final testing and verification of assumptions could be conducted.

*Institutional Space Policies and Guidelines.* Institutional space policies with respect to utilization and allocation were inherent in the development of the existing provincial space standards. However, the process of developing micro standards revealed that there were few institutional space policies in place and that the existing policies did not correspond to the policies set out by the provincial space standards. It was recognized that space management policies could set an institutional framework for the decision-making process associated with the allocation of physical resources and that they could be a consistent and equitable base that would become familiar to faculty and department administrators and academic staff. Therefore, institutional space policies obtained at the assistant vice-presidential and provostial level were incorporated into the customized micro space standards.

Because institutional policies set the ground rules for the utilization of space, it was vital to understand how they meshed with the policies implicit in the space formulas. For example, although the COU formulas for determining graduate student office-type space allocated 43 square feet per FTE graduate student in a department, the institution adopted a policy to provide office workstations only to resident graduate students doing thesis work and students participating in teaching or research activities. The percentage of such students actually varies from one department to another, so calculating space by FTE would be misleading; instead, the requirement for space is based on demonstrated need. In addition to this general institutional policy, it was recognized that some flexibility was required for certain academic programs, such as engineering, that had programmatic requirements exceeding the 43 square feet standard work station and that could not be adequately served by the institutional policy of housing some but not all graduate students.

*Existing Facility Information.* The space inventory is the element most frequently associated with a space analysis exercise, and a review of it is usually one of the first steps. It describes the current facilities in terms of the number, type, and size of rooms allocated to each department. However, the utilization descriptors used in space inventories are generally part of a coded structure that is limited to its ability to describe the activities that occur in a room. Therefore, for a comprehensive analysis to take place, additional information must be obtained in order to gain a complete understanding of a department's resources and requirements. The types of additional data collected are usually defined by the customized space standards. Some of these are detailed in the next section. In one of the final steps of a space analysis exercise, the space inventory, sorted into space categories using the same definitions as the space standards, is compared with the space requirements generated by application of the micro and sometimes the macro space formulas. The updating and augmentation of departmental space inventories is a necessary step not only in the space analysis process but in the development of space standards. For example, existing institutional averages can be calculated. As stated earlier, the COU formula has a space factor of 140 square feet for faculty offices, but the actual space factor (or average) at the University of Toronto is 168 square feet, a reality that application of the customized institutional space standards takes into account.

*Dialogue with User Groups.* The key to establishing an accurate assessment of program needs is a clear understanding of the day-to-day activities, both instructional and research, within the department. This understanding is accomplished during the information-gathering phase of the space analysis process. The data-gathering phase is data intensive and requires a considerable amount of dialogue with the department being analyzed.

Often, departmental representatives and other users have never been exposed to the space planning process, and they have little knowledge about space standards, utilization requirements, the institutional process for capital development, or the process for allocation of funds related to capital development. Therefore, the participation of users in a constructive manner throughout the information-gathering stage is an essential element. To refine the space analysis process, a handbook of policies and procedures has been developed to acquaint persons involved in space planning exercises with the prevailing rules regarding space allocation in the institution and with the analysis process itself. The handbook provides an opportunity to display all relevant space information, such as committee terms of reference, senate policies, capital development policies, and so forth. Although the handbook is not designed so that departments can analyze their own space requirements, it will assist them in understanding the process and in defining their activities in spatial terms.

The handbook is divided into four sections. Three provide background information, and one outlines the work to be done in a space analysis. The first section describes the planning process, and the roles played by different institutional administrative groups are outlined. The second section describes the provincial space classification scheme used in the university's space inventory and the provincial macro space standards. The third section outlines the space standards and guidelines currently in use at the University of Toronto—the standards and guidelines that were developed as a result of the evaluation of provincial space standards and the review of institutional space policies. The fourth section contains detailed descriptions of the data required for an analysis of a department's space requirements.

When a users committee is set up, it meets with representatives of the Office of the Assistant Vice-President, Planning and the Office of Space Management. The goal of the committee is to produce a users report that formulates a space plan for improvement or enlargement of the division's space as required by its academic program. The committee uses the last section of the handbook as a guide in collecting all the relevant data needed for analysis.

Three types of data are collected: space inventory data, hard data on routine utilization, and soft data that identify unique characteristics of the department. The characteristics of each kind of data are carefully defined so that they can be integrated with the institutional space standards and guidelines.

*Space Inventory Data.* The departmental space inventory and related floor plans are updated. Other data not normally carried on the space inventory can be collected during discussions with departmental representatives and incorporated into the inventory. These data can vary from descriptive information about staff positions and functions to classifications of teaching and research laboratories developed specifically for space analysis exercises. The aim is to have a totally integrated package of current data at the end of this phase. The information will be used to create a spreadsheet that will eventually display both the existing facilities and the required facilities.

*Hard Data.* The department is provided with a listing of data, one set for each of the five space categories, needed for an analysis of its facilities requirements. The data collected are then organized by category and existing facilities and held in worksheets (made much easier by use of computerized spreadsheet programs). Some of these data can be reconciled with those held on central data bases. In fact, the gathering of these data can start as an update and expansion of data from a central source. Following is a sample of the data that might be requested in three of the categories.

For classrooms, by course:

- Course name and number
- Term taught
- Number of sections
- Section enrollments
- Number of times each section meets per week
- Duration of each section meeting
- Day and time each section meets
- Type of furniture and room layout required by section (lecture or seminar)
- Equipment required (blackout curtains, overhead projector, and so forth).

For teaching laboratories, by laboratory:

- Data similar to those just listed for classrooms, but organized by lab type (for example, chemical engineering, analytical chemistry labs, first-year basic chemistry labs, organic chemistry, computer labs, nuclear labs, thermodynamics and kinetics labs, unit operations labs)
- List of associated lab support rooms.

For research laboratories, departments list the following by principal investigator, investigator group, or laboratory type, whichever is most appropriate:

- Name of the principal investigator
- Name or type of project
- Room number(s) or laboratory(ies) assigned
- Laboratory type (for example, benchtop lab, floor space lab, computer lab, electronic lab, large equipment lab, heavy equipment lab)
- Size and type of research team
- Number of desk and study spaces for graduate students within the laboratory
- Associated support rooms.

*Soft Data.* Requirements for facilities to house department activities that cannot be easily measured numerically must also be addressed in discussions with the participating department. The aim is to achieve a clear understanding of all facets of the department, its academic program, and its current facilities. To facilitate these discussions, a list of questions has been created, one set of questions for each of the five categories of space. The questions included in these sets vary from one situation to another. They are meant only to encourage discussion and to ensure that no requirement has been overlooked. The members of the users group are advised to raise any issues not covered by the questions that they feel might have an effect on their spatial requirements.

For teaching laboratories, the questions can include, to what extent is each lab required for unscheduled student use? Will the course offerings and section enrollments maintain the status quo of the terms analyzed, or is there a proposed and approved plan for changing the academic program? If the project involves new or renovated facilities, what are the preferred laboratory capacities and lab layouts? If the project involves existing space, what are the physical and functional limitations that affect existing and proposed activities? Are there other compatible courses using the same furnishings, layout, and equipment that could be taught in the same laboratory? Are there any peculiar timetable or scheduling habits or constraints that affect the efficient use of space from Monday to Friday, 9:00 A.M. to 6:00 P.M. (for example, three-hour labs, lecture schedules, additional setup time)? Are there any special support space requirements integral to the function of the lab that could be located in centralized space? How much space is the department willing to dedicate to dead storage?

For research laboratories, to the questions just listed for teaching labs that are relevant to research labs can be added, Will the research activities remain at the same level for the upcoming year, or are adjustments to funding levels expected? How much undergraduate teaching or preparation for undergraduate teaching occurs within these research labs?

For offices, the questions include, Is there a significant difference between the number of FTE budgeted faculty and the number of people actually requiring office accommodation, such as visiting faculty, professors emeriti, postdoctoral fellows, and status-only appointments? How many graduate students have a demonstrated need for office accommodation as opposed to alternate accommodation in a lab or study space? That is, how many are working as research assistants or teaching assistants? Are there research projects within the department that require office-type accommodation in addition to accommodations for the principal investigator? Is there associated equipment or special nonlaboratory activities that require office space? Are there staff who need offices larger than 130 square feet, and for what purpose? Is space to be provided by reallocation, renovation, or new construction? If a project is to be in existing space, what are the limiting physical and functional factors? Is there an anticipated or approved plan to increase or decrease the number of faculty, staff, or students within the department?

The lists of routine utilization data and the questions that are used to encourage discussion with the departments are never viewed as ironclad. They are guides, and they vary with the characteristics of the department being analyzed and the nature of the space program being developed.

### Analysis, Application, and Comparison

The analysis phase of the process applies the customized micro space standards and the established institutional space policies to the data collected by the users committee. This analysis can take any of several forms, depending on the purpose of the project and the categories of space involved in the project.

However, before the nominal space requirement is calculated, each component of the micro space standards and formulas for each category of space required by the department is quickly reviewed one last time. This review is similar to the evaluation done on the provincial space standards, but this time it is based on detailed knowledge of a particular department and especially on the information revealed in the soft data discussions:

- *Input measure:* Is it in fact the most representative generator? Are there inclusions or exclusions that would improve it as a measuring tool? Is there an approved or anticipated change that should also be included in the study?
- *Area component of the space factor:* Is it an accurate measure of the amount of space needed to accommodate the type of furniture, equipment, or activity that will be housed? If the project involves new construction, does it represent an institutional standard, or if the project involves existing space, does it match the current facilities?
- *Utilization component of the space factor:* Does it represent an accepted institutional or faculty standard? Does it recognize the requirements of the academic program of this particular department?

Any necessary adjustments are made to the standards, and the routine utilization data—the so-called hard data—are then used to calculate the space formulas. This final modification is not to imply that the department can have a wish list that can alter the space standards but that each space requirement is generated by a careful study of all the department's activities. It has been validated by demonstrated and approved need, and it has been reflected in the process used to develop the departmental space program.

The results of the analysis are compared with the existing facilities identified in the updated inventory. This comparison highlights any inefficiencies of space utilization that new construction or renovation might correct or that reallocation of existing space might adjust. The analyses are presented in detail or in summary on spreadsheets and generally contain the following:

- *Existing facilities:* room number, room area, and use description
- *Nominal allocation:* the space required to accommodate the existing and approved activities of a department as calculated by the customized university micro standards and formulas
- *Additional allocation:* additional space requirements that reflect a demonstrated need by the department for accommodation that is in excess of or less than that specified by the standards
- *Other users:* space required to accommodate other independent or noninstitutional users where approved
- *Anticipated growth:* space required for activities that are planned but not yet approved (kept separate from the allocation required to house existing and approved activities)
- *Proposed allocation:* used when the project is a reallocation of existing space requiring a room-by-room match of staff and function, or in cases where a portion of a department's activities are to remain in place but the rooms are not standard size.

As a final step, the provincial system formula may be calculated for comparison purposes. Discrepancies are noted, reviewed, and, if required, explained, as in capital projects. Comparison of the provincial macro formulas with the adjusted micro formulas does not always produce consistent results. Because the adjusted formulas now recognize the uniqueness of individual departments, any one department may generate more of one kind of space or less of another than the provincial formulas do. Departments will also vary in the proportional amounts of space generated for the same category of space. However, because the micro space standards have been carefully customized for the institution, the reasoning for variances from the provincial standards are easy to explain.

Micro space standards are intended for use at the departmental level during analysis of a single department. The ability to use them for all the departments on a campus is limited only by the time frame and the staff available. The results of an individual analysis or group of departmental analyses can be folded into the existing campus space inventory, thereby measuring the effect of a project on the institution's space and on its entitlement generated by the provincial space formula.

## Conclusion

An established, accepted process of space analysis that recognizes individual departmental requirements provides a consistent approach to the task of finding solutions for space allocation problems. The development of this process necessarily requires an initial commitment of time and effort from the offices responsible for space standards, space inventory, and university policies that relate to space management. However, the final product is an objective procedure that, by providing supportive guidelines, minimizes disruptions arising from sensitive territorial and economic concerns.

It is to be expected that changes will be made in the macro standards currently in use in North America. A number of jurisdictions are now involved in reviews of their system space standards. In Ontario, the COU (1972, 1978, 1988) *Building Blocks* Standards, which were reviewed by a task force in recent years, are being scrutinized once again. Nevertheless, as system standards will of necessity continue to be based on averages and generalizations, the requirement for planners to respond to allocation crises and to plan at a micro level will necessitate the use of standards adapted for their own institutional use. As funding agencies increasingly require institutions to use macro system standards, the new challenge will be to develop processes for linking macro standards with micro standards and justifying any differences between the two.

## References

Council of Ontario Universities. *Building Blocks: Background Studies on the Development of a Capital Formula for Ontario. Vol. 1: Report of the Task Force Space and Utilization.* Toronto: Council of Ontario Universities, 1972.

Council of Ontario Universities. *Building Blocks. Vol. 6: Report of the Subcommittee Revisions to Building Blocks.* Toronto: Council of Ontario Universities, 1978.

Council of Ontario Universities. *Building Blocks. Vol. 7: Final Report of the Task Force to Review COU Space Standards.* Toronto: Council of Ontario Universities, 1988.

*Gail Milgrom is space information coordinator at the University of Toronto and a member of the Council of Ontario Universities Committee on Space Standards and Reporting.*

*Elizabeth Sisam is the research and planning officer for campus and facilities planning and an architect at the University of Toronto. Together with Gail Milgrom, she has written and spoken on the subject of facility management and space planning in postsecondary institutions.*

*This chapter describes a multipart strategy for ensuring
adequate funding of building repair.*

# The Politics of Budgeting
# for Deferred Maintenance

*Laura E. Saunders*

The funding of maintenance projects has been a growing problem for
higher education, as for all public-sector agencies, throughout the last
twenty years. Articles calling attention to the crumbling condition of
roads, bridges, dams, and highways have verified the massive underfunding of maintenance and repair at all levels of government. In higher
education, long lists of deferred maintenance projects are used in budget
justification; accelerating deterioration and reduced funding are two
causes frequently cited. In addition, the tendency of many institutions to
put a higher priority on the maintenance of academic programs than on
painting, making structural repairs, fixing roofs, and closing leaks has
contributed to the seriousness of the situation. Those charged with weigh-
ing priorities between operating and capital needs in recent years have
usually given preference to operating needs. However, maintenance cannot be put off indefinitely, and institutions are beginning to have to deal
with the accumulated backlog of deferred maintenance.

A recent study of higher education (Helpern, 1987) estimated the
underfunding of maintenance for higher education at about $2 billion.
The Association of Physical Plant Administrators of Colleges and Universities (1989) estimates that the cost of updating and repairing out-

H. H. Kaiser (ed.). *Planning and Managing Higher Education Facilities.*
New Directions for Institutional Research, no. 61. San Francisco: Jossey-Bass, Spring 1989.

moded, decayed, and obsolete buildings on the nation's campuses could run to $70 billion.

Planning for deferred maintenance and developing detailed estimates and plans for restoring the campus will occupy the attention of administrators at all levels in the next few years. Yet, the problems go beyond the merely technical ones of identifying the needed repairs and developing plans for meeting them. The planning process involves decisions on how best to allocate limited funds. Most campuses have long lists of deferred maintenance projects: buildings systems that need replacement, electrical systems that require updating and added capacity, roofs that have failed or are about to, building layouts that do not meet the needs of researchers or teachers. The existence of these project lists, which have been a feature of campus budget building for a number of years, has not aided in establishing priorities for the addressing of deferred maintenance needs.

Other ways of creating a consensus about the urgency of the need to begin addressing deferred maintenance systematically must be developed. The decision to put renovating, updating, and repair needs ahead of other needs on campus is similar to other campus priority-setting problems, and, in the end, it is a political problem as much as it is a technical problem. For private institutions where capital and operating funds are not dedicated, choices conflict—faculty salaries versus roof repairs, for instance. In public institutions where funds are often dedicated to either capital or operating purposes, the choices are less clearly posed, but institutional leaders have to address the question of relative priority in defining the institution's needs to funding authorities. Without internal agreement about the relative importance of repair and renovation, efforts to obtain these funds from outside are not likely to be convincing.

Over the last ten years, the University of Washington has begun to address its deferred maintenance needs systematically through a multipart strategy that includes building an externally reinforced consensus, internal monitoring, a review and priority-setting system, and a conscious budget strategy that separates needs for deferred maintenance from projects that serve teaching and research directly. This strategy has allowed the university to increase its spending for deferred maintenance projects from $15 million in 1981-1983 to $38 million in 1987-1989. Each element of this strategy played an important political as well as technical role in reinforcing the priority to be given to the repair and updating of building systems.

## Context

The capital and operating budgets of the University of Washington, a large public university, are biennial. For a number of years, the university generated funds for capital projects, including renovation and repair, through its own funds: timber trust land income, indirect cost recovery, building use fees, and earnings from the lease of the university's original site in downtown Seattle. Maintenance projects were funded primarily out of the operating budget, based on a physical plant formula agreed upon interinstitutionally that was similar to those in use in many public institutions. The formula provided dollar measures of need based on ratios divided according to type of construction and age. However, by the end of the 1970s, the realities of economic decline in the state led to four years of cuts in the operating budget, during which general fund tax support for the operating budget was reduced, and the funds previously dedicated to capital budgets were diverted to the operating budget. Program expenses, faculty salaries, and other operating budget items were paid for with former capital budget sources of funds. No new buildings were built, and a regular renovation schedule for older buildings was ignored. With reduced funds for both capital and operating budget support, major projects were not started, either, as small repair projects grew to larger scale.

By 1983, it had become clear that reduced operating budget expenditures for maintenance and a sharply lower level of capital budget renovation were having their effect on campus buildings. Story after story surfaced about leaky roofs, inadequate plumbing systems, and building electrical services that could no longer support computers and scientific instruments. Reduced repairs money, coupled with the complete absence of new building projects and a steady increase in research activity, led to a growing realization that the condition of existing buildings was beginning to be a major factor affecting what could be done in the buildings.

Other institutions across the nation, less affected by economic downturn, continued new construction in the late 1970s and early 1980s and were meeting the technological needs of research by moving the technologically sophisticated programs into new facilities, which left the older buildings available for less demanding use. At the University of Washington, there were neither new buildings into which sophisticated research could be moved nor money to update old buildings in which such work could be housed. Competition to retain existing faculty and attract new faculty increasingly hinged on the amount and quality of the capital facilities available.

## External Consensus

Two major efforts were undertaken to create an external consensus in favor of increased spending on building renovation and deferred maintenance. The first was the product of the Washington Roundtable, a group of business executives in the state who, at the suggestion of higher education leaders from the university, undertook a study of the condition of university buildings and the administration of its maintenance program. The intent was to use nonuniversity staff and commercial or industrial standards to develop an independent and objective report on the condition of the institution's facilities. Less intensive surveys of other higher education institutions in Washington were also conducted by the same teams with the same standards, but because of the greater age and sophistication of its facilities, the major effort focused on the university.

External studies of higher education are not new, either in Washington or in the country as a whole. They can resemble expose investigations when they bring in outside experts and reveal inefficient management and corruption. In contrast, the Washington Roundtable study of maintenance at the university was based on the concept that industry could bring its knowledge to bear on the university's problems, substantiate the university's claims that building limitations were a serious problem, and provide an independent voice that the legislature could trust in setting budget priorities.

The Washington Roundtable study used a team of building experts from major corporations around the state, whose services were donated by their companies. The experts were on campus for about three months, and they brought in additional experts to survey roofs, look at the outsides of buildings, and develop an overall list of building maintenance needs. In addition, they reviewed the management of the physical plant unit that administered maintenance programs. The Roundtable report, released in June 1984, contained the results of a survey of facilities conducted in ninety-seven large campus buildings that accounted for almost eight million gross square feet. The survey found major problems in a number of aspects of the buildings and emphasized the prevalence of water damage through building exteriors and roofs. Although there were differences between the Roundtable's approach and the more detailed summary maintained by university staff, the total magnitude of the needs was similar. By fall 1984, prior to the opening of the legislative session, stories of leaky roofs and crumbling buildings were appearing in the local press.

State government, in part in response to this publicity but also out of a growing awareness that similar problems existed in other state facilities, issued budget instructions that emphasized deferred maintenance needs and building renovation over new construction. The university's request followed this emphasis. The report called for an expenditure of $18 million to address immediate facility restoration needs at the university and suggested a higher ongoing level of preventive maintenance spending.

The second major effort to develop and strengthen an external consensus followed on the earlier Roundtable study and involved a survey, completed in spring 1988, of all science and engineering facilities on the campus. After some years of emphasizing the piecemeal renovation of older buildings due to legislative reluctance to endorse new construction, it became apparent that the university's aging laboratory facilities were not adequate to retain existing faculty and attract new hires. When the costs of renovating and equipping a 6,000-square-foot organic chemistry lab approached $3 million, the wisdom of renovation to meet the needs for science seemed questionable. A team of two consulting firms was hired by the university and charged with developing a detailed survey of university science and engineering facilities. In order to determine whether the university's science labs were adequate, the consultants were asked to visit other institutions with which the university competes for faculty to see the state of the art of science labs. The consulting firms provided teams of building system, laboratory, and architectural consultants, and their study was divided into four parts: a survey of competitive institutions for the condition and changes anticipated in their facilities, a survey of university science and engineering buildings, a review of the growth and change anticipated by academic fields, and a survey of potential sites on campus for the construction of new facilities.

As the report developed and as the analysis of the potential of existing buildings for retrofitting and upgrading progressed, it became clear that renovation was no longer feasible and that a massive program of new construction would be needed if the university was to remain viable as a major research university. The consultant's report was then used to support the university's capital budget as a comprehensive, in-depth survey of competitive needs and existing conditions.

While the strategy of using external consultants to support university budget requests is not new, it has seldom involved an effort on such a large scale. The report on science and engineering facilities received wide publicity when it was completed. It was used to brief university regents and legislative and executive branch leaders, and it was distributed extensively as part of the university's capital budget request.

**Internal Monitoring, Review, and Priority Setting**

Nevertheless, external consensus about the importance of spending for repair, renovation, and new construction would not have been successful in the absence of an internally agreed upon system for setting priorities. During the late 1970s, the university's physical plant administrators, along with budget and planning analysts, became increasingly dissatisfied with the way in which capital repair and renewal projects were being planned and scheduled for funding. At budget development time, lists of needs were compiled to serve as the basis for review and eventual inclusion in the request. When the legislature acted, the resulting funds were then in principle applied to the lists, but the projects actually funded were often quite different from those listed as of highest priority. There was a general feeling that getting a project on the list and having the project funded depended more on who requested the project than on the inherent severity of the problem.

The solution to this rather haphazard compilation of lists and allocation of funds was the development of a program that was eventually named the Preventive Repair and Maintenance (PRAM) program, and the list of projects with which it was associated was called the PRAM list. The PRAM list approach started at the University of Washington with a series of meetings aimed at determining a more rational and defensible way of determining relative needs for funding. Because officials from academic affairs, facilities offices, and plant engineering all were struggling with the problem of developing a better system, the result was not a one-dimensional or one-criteria solution. The PRAM program evolved from an organizational context in which multiunit committees had already been used extensively in developing budget recommendations.

In theory, assessments of deferred maintenance needs usually assume that there is a complete and detailed building survey. While members of the planning group that eventually developed the PRAM program realized the utility of having complete surveys, they also understood that in the University of Washington setting they were unlikely ever to have enough money to commission these surveys. Because only limited funds have been available for all capital-related projects in recent years, the choice had been to concentrate on the repair work itself as more pressing than surveys. Any approach to a more rational and defensible system could not assume the funding necessary for having complete surveys made. Even the work done for the science and engineering study and the Roundtable report did not cover all structures on campus or all aspects of the structures that were surveyed. Piecemeal surveys did exist. An asbestos survey had been conducted in the mid 1980s, a survey of fire code compliance had been done in the early 1980s, and lists of the improvements needed to enhance program function had been compiled and submitted by academic department chairs as part of the two-year budget process. What did not exist was a way of deciding what was most important—repairing leaking roofs, fitting out a new lab, or updating a building ventilation system. Because funding was so limited and so few new facilities were being built, the pressure was on to make the best decisions possible. (In campuses where funds were more available, such difficult choices did not have to be made, or they could be bypassed by constructing new facilities for the most sophisticated uses.)

The innovative approach embodied in the PRAM process was not the list itself but the ranking system that was embodied in it. The PRAM list process began by having the chief plant engineer collect all lists of projects from all relevant campus sources: environmental health and safety, academic unit heads, plant engineering and utility specialists, and so forth. These lists were merged, the duplicates were eliminated, and each project remaining was rated according to five criteria: how serious a code problem the condition involved, how substantial a liability issue it entailed, the effect it had on the usefulness of the building, the potential it created for further deterioration, and its impact on the operating budget. Every project was rated on each criterion. Ratings ranged between one (relatively minor) to seven (most serious). For the first round in the PRAM process, the ratings were assigned by a subcommittee consisting of academic unit representatives, one safety and health representative, the chief plant engineer, and a general facilities office manager. A larger group of senior-level staff reviewed the final request and recommended the budget request amounts.

The rating reflected a negative approach—what is the effect if nothing is done?—and it reflected differences in the seriousness of the problem across criteria. Although the five ratings could have been added together to obtain a total severity rank for the first several biennia in which the system was applied, the total of the ratings that each project obtained was not used as the sole determinant of inclusion on the list of projects to be funded. Initially, projects that had liability or code problems with a rating of six or seven were placed at the top of the list. The decision to emphasize reduction of the university's exposure to liability by correcting as many of these high-risk projects as possible was ratified by the senior management group to whom the subcommittee reported. It is possible, and was initially considered a desirable feature, that different weights be assigned to each of the criteria. In practice, the individual criteria have never been weighted in the eight years in which the PRAM system has been used.

In addition to the ratings, the list, which is computerized, includes cost estimates for fixing the problem, a categorization of the general type of problem (for example, building systems, plumbing, roofs, exterior repairs), a very brief description, the building name, and the department that occupies the space, if applicable.

In the course of developing a budget request and spending plan from the PRAM system, several other analyses are done. Because the PRAM list is easy to manipulate, totals are compiled for individual buildings, and buildings with large numbers of problems are reviewed individually to determine whether renovation of the entire building is preferable to trying to fix all the individual problems. If a building has several kinds of problems but the magnitude of the problems is not sufficient to justify renovation of the entire building, coordination of work can still result in savings. For example, by combining fire safety work and asbestos, disruption to building inhabitants can be reduced. Prior to the PRAM list, separate offices scheduled their building projects separately, and it was not unusual, although it was frustrating for a building's users, to have one crew after another come through the building with a sequence of repair jobs that could all have been done at once. For instance, the city of Seattle mandated an extensive fire code project that required the updating of all university buildings, and asbestos abatement work frequently had to be done as well. Had there been no systematic review of all projects through the PRAM collection and ranking process, building occupants might have found themselves subjected to month after month of continuous construction.

The PRAM list is updated and maintained by an interdepartmental group that reviews each project, adds new ones, and verifies cost estimates and severity ratings on a quarterly basis. The group reports to the head of the facilities management group. It consists of academic unit representatives, the chief plant engineer, environmental health and safety office staff, and capital budget managers. The group is informal, having no formal charge or specified membership, and it is convened on a quarterly basis by the chief plant engineer. Additional staff are invited on an as-needed basis when specialized expertise is required. Just before a biennial budget request is developed, the PRAM list gets intense scrutiny by the interdepartmental group to ensure that all relevant projects have been included and that cost estimates for repairs are up to date. When there is agreement on the entire list, the budget request (or list of projects to be done) is developed from the PRAM list and forwarded to the campus committee that finally approves all capital funding. The recommendations of the interdepartmental committee are only occasionally modified by this capital budget committee.

The use of an interdepartmental committee results in a consensus about the ratings and the order of importance of the projects. Once the relative priorities for potential funding have been agreed to, a detailed review of the most deficient projects is made. Project scopes are refined, and detailed cost estimates are prepared.

Although the PRAM list is primarily a management tool used for deciding on the projects that will be done, it also provides an ongoing estimate of the total deferred maintenance need on campus, and it makes it possible to see from budget cycle to budget cycle whether the funding of building repair is keeping pace with deterioration. The existence of such a list and the process for maintaining and reviewing it have served to reassure the campus community and senior management that their needs have been evaluated fairly. That is, the list of projects to be done has become relatively objective. The methodology behind the PRAM process and the lists themselves have been shared with other state agencies and with state budget officers as examples of the university's approach to the management of capital budgets. At least one other institution in the state has initiated a similar process.

The PRAM list has some weaknesses: The ratings given on each criterion are arbitrary and subject to challenge. The solutions to particular problems agreed to at one point in time may persist beyond their useful life. For instance, the PRAM list may have a cost estimate that assumes a type of roofing material that is no longer available, and hence the estimate is undependable. Given a list of three hundred or more projects, it is not possible to be sure that there are up-to-date design drawings and cost estimates for each project. The PRAM process provides for integrating and comparing projects that support academic program needs with projects that replace building systems, such as ventilation, although it has not been widely used in this application. It is less useful in a context where there are ample funds, and careful choices are not necessary.

## Separating Deferred Maintenance from Program Projects

The third element of the deferred maintenance strategy developed for the University of Washington addressed the competition for capital funds between capital projects related to program function and capital projects related to repair, renovation, and restoration. This competition is a microcosm of larger conflict between support for academic programs and support for ancillary and business services. Should a project to add state-of-the-art cooling capacity to a research lab in order to make a new kind of research possible have higher priority than replacing uninsulated office or classroom windows with insulated windows? Should roof repair take priority over subdividing a large room to provide faculty with offices?

The problem of choosing between these two kinds of projects—building repair and academic needs—was compounded at the university because the state of Washington had provided a budget category that included funding that could be used for either. These so-called minor repairs projects did not have to be described in advance, and, although they were subject to state public works processes, in most cases they did not come under the same scrutiny as a larger project, such as complete renovation of a building or construction of a new building. This category of projects, variously called *minor works, small projects,* or *emergency repairs,* provided the flexibility needed in an era in which there were no new buildings and there was little in the way of ongoing entire-building renovation. However, the fact that two sets of actors were involved in making decisions about the use of these funds, one for each type of project—deans and faculty for programmatic projects, facilities engineers and plant personnel for building repair—impaired the usefulness of these funds for addressing the deferred maintenance problem. Over several biennia, the competition between program needs and building system repair needs became acute, and because the building system needs were generally less obvious, they were often left unfunded in favor of program objectives.

The competition itself was destructive, since each set of actors cast doubt on the legitimacy of the claims advanced by the other set. The result was a climate of mistrust in the process.

Growing out of consensus in the state that deferred maintenance was a major problem, the state legislature's instructions for the 1985–1987 budget allowed for the division of minor works projects into two separate appropriations, one for program and one for deferred maintenance and building repair. With segregated requests, the competition for the funds was reduced, and it became possible to program funds consistently to address the projects on the PRAM list. The existence of the PRAM approach at the university was a key to the decision of the state budget office to allow the division of funds, because it was clear to the state that an orderly process for the review of needs and the establishment of priorities was in place. The university initiated the request for separate funding, and the state agreed to it, thus putting an end to the destructive competition. This was one case in which suboptimizing proved to be the best solution for the institutional decision-making process.

## Lessons Learned

The University of Washington experience has evolved over the last ten years as one way of approaching the difficult political problems involved in ensuring an adequate level of funding for building system problems and deferred maintenance. This approach is specific to the context of the state and the university, and it draws heavily on local practices. It was developed in response to a historically specific lack of funds for building surveys and whole building projects. However, it has three characteristics that should be applicable in other locales.

First, it relied on external confirmation to back up campus assessment of problems. The role of the Washington Roundtable's report in confirming what university officials had been saying all along was one key. Use of an independent body to verify the magnitude and severity of the problem created a political climate that supported spending for the unglamorous projects. A subsequent survey of science and engineering facilities by external experts emphasized the university's technical facilities.

Second, it had an internal management system in place. The PRAM list process provided the necessary confirmation that problems would be addressed in an orderly way and that there was a priority-setting system that enabled projects to be compared and related. Once funding was available, the PRAM approach provided a rational basis for deciding how it was to be spent.

Third, it reduced the conflict over the use of funds. Before the system was put into place, building needs usually came out second best when they had to compete with program needs for the funds that were available. By segregating funds, we could address building needs in a systematic fashion, with a degree of deliberation that contention over the total level of funds did not permit. Over time, it remains to be seen whether segregated funds will be optimal for the institution as a whole, but in this particular setting it is clear that reducing the competition was essential, since it ratified the legitimacy of the process.

To summarize, the University of Washington experience illustrates that capital budgeting is not solely a technical problem but one that involves a complex interaction of adequate technical information and strategy planning.

## Conclusion

The key element of the University of Washington experience is the PRAM process, which grew out of an institutional approach to budgeting for capital projects that relied heavily on small interdepartmental committees. Developing fairly complete lists and developing the willingness to engage in the effort required to agree on priorities required a substantial commitment of time, at least in the initial stages. Another key feature in the acceptance ultimately accorded the PRAM process was that it produced a data base that was easy to manipulate. Ratings could be reviewed and changed as necessary, and what-if budgets could be produced. Totals for all projects over a certain priority level or for all projects of a certain type could be generated. Projects in certain sectors of the campus could be looked at together. The actual process of applying the PRAM list to the development of a budget request or to decisions about how to spend the funding that was available was enhanced by the ability that it gave participants to look at the total project list from a number of perspectives. In the end, this capital budgeting process has an element of a political, decision-making process, but the fact that it is founded on an agreed upon list and ranking process has reduced the conflict involved in reaching a final determination and increased public confidence that the most serious problems on the campus are being addressed.

## References

Association of Physical Plant Administrators of Colleges and Universities, National Association of Colleges and University Business Officers, and Coopers & Lybrand. *The Decaying American Campus: A Ticking Time Bomb*. Alexandria, Va.: Association of Physical Plant Administrators of Colleges and Universities, 1989.

Helpern, D. P. *The State of College and University Facilities*. New York: Society for College and University Planning, 1987.

Washington Business Roundtable. *Report on Washington State's Higher Education System: An Industry Survey of Maintenance Needs*. Seattle, Wash.: Washington Business Roundtable, 1984.

*Laura E. Saunders is director of planning and capital budget at the University of Washington in Seattle. She is a past president of the Association for Institutional Research.*

*How much should an institution be spending or putting aside over the long run to preserve the value of its plant assets to its evolving mission?*

# Financial Planning for Plant Assets

## John A. Dunn, Jr.

The Association of Physical Plant Administrators of Colleges and Universities (APPA) and the National Association of College and University Business Officers (NACUBO) found this year that U.S. higher education faced a $20 billion backlog in urgent facility repair needs and that the total costs for capital renewal and replacement on campus may run as high as $60 to $70 billion (Association of Physical Plant Administrators . . . , 1989).

Similarly, a National Science Foundation (1988) study showed that only a little over half of all colleges and universities described their current research space as sufficient either to support all their research needs or as sufficient to support most research needs. Twenty-three percent of the research space was found to require limited repair and renovation, and 16 percent to require major repair and renovation. Even more significant, the National Science Foundation (1988, p. xiv) found that "the amount of space to be repaired/renovated in 1988 and 1989 (9 percent of existing space) represents only a portion of the space needing repair and renovation (R&R). Based on the costs of the reported R&R projects, it is estimated that about $3.60 in needed R&R is being deferred for every $1.00 in R&R [that] is planned."

American higher education has failed to protect and enhance the value of its facilities assets. The causes are multiple and complex, but the

H. H. Kaiser (ed.). *Planning and Managing Higher Education Facilities.*
New Directions for Institutional Research, no. 61. San Francisco: Jossey-Bass, Spring 1989.

result is clear. As the issue has come to popular attention in recent years, many institutions and some state systems have begun to try to catch up. However, it is as difficult to do so as it is for an overweight middle-aged man to restore vigorous good health by frenetic dieting and exercise, and it is just as unlikely to succeed over the long run. Massive short-term injections of cash may fix up some critical problems, but they may simply make one feel better today at the cost of being painfully sore tomorrow, especially if the cash comes from borrowing to be repaid from future operating revenues. To continue the health analogy but shift it a little, the cure is more likely to come in the realization that we are all alcoholics with respect to our attention to plant upkeep, far too easily tempted by other budget considerations. We need a clear, long-term rule to live by and a determination to stick to it.

## Some Terminology and a Context

In presenting the results of the APPA/NACUBO study, Sean Rush (1988) likened institutional plant maintenance and renovation to a family's upkeep of a car. Routine maintenance, he said, is like periodic replacement of the tires, changing the spark plugs, changing the oil. These expenditures are important to keep the car running smoothly, to minimize wear, and to keep it safe. Optimum schedules for these services are provided by the manufacturer. However, if money is tight, there is a temptation to postpone them, at least for a while. Deferred maintenance represents a backlog of costs that hide continuing deterioration and that must be met. For example, the oil gets grittier and grittier, and it will eventually do serious damage. If the expenditures are delayed too long, they create urgent needs. When the tires wear down to the fabric, they have to be replaced, or there is serious risk to the car and the occupants. After a period of years, capital renewal is needed: That is, it is necessary to replace the car. Keeping it going with maintenance expenditures becomes impossible or overly costly. However, the family sometimes discovers that its requirements have changed: There may be children now, and replacing the Volkswagen beetle will not do when a van is needed.

Rush used the analogy effectively to clarify the concepts used in the APPA/NACUBO study. The survey focused on identifying expenditures on routine maintenance and on the magnitude of deferred maintenance (and especially of urgent needs maintenance) in colleges and universities throughout the country. The study also sought to determine what the capital renewal needs were for those institutions.

This chapter focuses on the financial planning aspects of these questions. In a family, routine automotive maintenance costs are usually paid out of current income. Occasionally, if funds are tight, one might borrow to meet urgent needs. The new car is seldom paid for out of current income. It is usually paid for over time, through savings or loans. Getting a bigger car or buying a second car when the need arises can put a real strain on the finances.

An institution faces the family's vehicle-care-and-replacement question, raised to a high degree of complexity: How much should it be spending or putting aside over the long run to preserve the value of its plant assets to its evolving mission?

Because the focus of this chapter diverges a bit from that of the APPA/NACUBO study I will distinguish here between expenditures on routine maintenance and expenditures on plant upkeep and renewal. In the former category are ordinary janitorial services, unplugging of drains, routine replacements of light bulbs, cleaning and caulking of gutters, and the like—expenditures that have a useful life measured in weeks or months but not in years. We will assume that these expenditures form part of the ordinary operating budget of the institution, that they are easily budgeted as ongoing activities, and that they present no great challenge for long-range financial planning. We can contrast routine maintenance with plant upkeep and renewal expenditures, which are the direct concern of this chapter. These range from roof replacement to upgrading the plumbing systems, from road repaving to bringing a chemistry laboratory up to new standards. These expenditures have a useful life of one or more years.

There is no agreement as to how much an institution should put aside to meet these costs. A great deal of important and productive work has been done on quantifying the extent of the deferred maintenance problem (Kaiser, 1984; Helpern, 1987; Association of Physical Plant Administrators . . . , 1989). We now know far better what institutions are spending on urgent needs and on capital replacement, and we have some estimates of the volume of upkeep and maintenance needed that has not been funded. Thoughtful procedures have been developed to help an institution audit the condition of its facilities (Kaiser, 1987). However, a commonly accepted conceptual approach to the problem of long-term financial planning that an institution should use in its efforts to protect the value of its plant assets as the institution itself evolves is still missing. Fortunately, the basic components of such a theory exist, and it remains only to bring them together and develop them into a practical approach. The balance of this chapter is dedicated to identifying and beginning to integrate the components of a new theory. Much remains to be done to translate this new theory into a workable model, and the one outlined here may not be the only new theory or the best. Nonetheless, the need for a new approach is clear.

**Approaches That Do Not Work**

Before we examine the components of a system that might work, we need to review the commonly used methods of estimating future spending on plant upkeep and renewal to see why they are unsatisfactory.

Some institutions simply take the amount that they spent in the preceding year for plant upkeep and renewal and put it in the budget for the following year, perhaps adding a few percent for inflation. This approach is tempting, especially in institutions with severely limited funds. However, it is wholly unsatisfactory as a planning guideline. There is no way of assuring that either the previous year's actual or the future year's budget has any relationship to the amount that is really required in order to maintain the current value of the plant assets or to adapt them to the changing needs of the institution.

A more common approach is to audit the condition of the physical plant, identify the projects that must be tackled over the next year or two, attach price tags, and incorporate that expenditure projection into the budget. One advantage of this approach is that a carefully done "on-the-ground" survey identifies specific problems that a theoretical approach will not. Another advantage is that real needs, once identified, can be prioritized. A difficulty with the approach is that it tends to focus on specific identifiable problems rather than on the overall level of funding that should be provided on a continuing basis over the long run to protect the plant assets. The set of problems identified in any given year may be well above or well below the ongoing level of funding needed. A second difficulty is that, because this approach inevitably looks at the present physical plant and focuses on maintaining its current functionality, it can miss the funding needed to adapt the plant continually to the evolving needs of the institution.

### First Component of a New Theory: Facility Subsystems

In recent years, a number of campuses have undertaken a much more sophisticated approach to the plant audit that takes the actual present condition of the plant into account and lays a theoretical base for anticipating future needs.

Each building on a campus can be thought of as consisting of a set of subsystems, such as roofing, elevators, and heating, ventilating, and air-conditioning (HVAC) systems. According to Hutson and Biedenweg (1982), facility subsystems have three characteristics: They collectively constitute the building, each subsystem has a definable useful life, and information on subsystem cost and performance is available. These authors identify the following subsystems from their experience at Stanford University: foundations and major vertical, floor, and roof structures; roofing; exterior cladding; interior partitions, interior finishes; elevators; plumbing; HVAC moving; HVAC static; electrical moving; electrical static; fire protection; and special equipment and miscellaneous.

Using facility subsystems as the unit of analysis, the maintenance planner can construct a projection of what is required to maintain facilities in good operating condition. First, the life cycle for each system in a particular building can be estimated. While there are some general life cycle expectations (for example, roofing should last between twenty-five and thirty years, interior finishes, between three and ten years), some consideration should be given to the type of facility involved. Interior finishes in a student union might well need replacement considerably more often than those in a faculty office building. A careful inspection of the condition of each subsystem in the building will indicate a likely next date of replacement or major repair, giving a starting point for the next life cycle of that subsystem.

The second step is to estimate the replacement cost of each of the subsystems in the building. These also will vary by type of building: The mechanical systems in a laboratory building will be much more expensive than those in a classroom facility.

Once the replacement cost, the life cycle, and the next repair or replacement date have been established for the building, a schedule can be laid out showing the work likely to be needed and the related costs for a period that extends many years into the future. Aggregating these estimates for all the facilities on campus will show the overall flow of funds that is likely to be needed. Expressed as a percentage of plant replacement cost, such calculations are likely to show a need for an annual expenditure of as high as 3.1 percent (Kaiser, 1982) or, more often, between 1.5 and 2.6 percent (Hutson and Biedenweg, 1982). Of course, the specific figure depends on the mix of types of facility on the campus and on the age and the time since last major repair of each building subsystem.

## Second Component of a New Theory: Financial Equilibrium Planning

Necessity being the mother of invention, the high-inflation years of the mid to late 1970s gave birth to the concepts of financial equilibrium planning (Hopkins and Massy, 1981). As long as inflation remained low, it was possible for a college budget planner to express his longer-range projections in current dollars. He or she knew that the actual numbers would escalate slowly, but the planner could assume that inflation would affect most revenue and expenditure items more or less equally. Thus, most financial planning could be straight-line extensions of the current situation, with modifications introduced by hand as needed for changes in student populations or other variables.

Higher inflation in the late 1970s quickly made it clear that not all variables changed at the same rate. Energy costs skyrocketed. Food costs stayed relatively low. Return on endowment assets grew only very slowly. The cost of library materials and equipment climbed rapidly. The aim of multiple-year budget planning had to be altered. It no longer gave security to balance this year's revenues and expenditures. To achieve financial equilibrium in current operations, it was essential to balance the rates of change of the revenue and expense variables.

Highly sophisticated approaches were developed for this task, culminating in the heavily mathematical series of tools and concepts advanced by Hopkins and Massy (1981). To embody the concepts and manage their application, new computer tools were developed that began to extend the applications of computer use to interested faculty members and administrators (Wyatt, Emery, and Landis, 1979). Computer modeling tools gained wide use, and they were quickly replaced as microcomputer spreadsheets became available.

College and university accounting practices account for institutional funds in four main categories: current funds, endowment funds, plant funds, and loan funds. These initial equilibrium planning tools pertained principally to the planning and management of current-year operations. A parallel development of more relevance to our present concern with plant assets took place during the 1970s with respect to the planning and management of endowment funds.

During the 1930s, 1940s, and 1950s, it was clearly and widely understood that prudent financial management of an endowment meant spending only the dividends and interest earned and keeping capital wisely invested. Investment in common stocks was risky, and it was to be approached with caution. Furthermore, many common stocks paid out only very low dividends, and operating managers needed more. Treasurers therefore often invested heavily in preferred stock and bonds that paid out reasonable returns and protected their principal. The long bull market of the 1950s began to erode the general agreement on that investment philosophy. Common stocks grew enormously in value. By the middle to late 1960s, the received wisdom was that (except where prohibited by law or "prudent man" rules) one should invest aggressively for "total return" (dividends and interest plus both realized and unrealized capital gains). The investment manager then paid out to the operating budget a portion of the total return and left the balance in the endowment. While the change in principle was liberating to endowment managers, it opened the door to enthusiasts who felt that they could earn 15 percent or more in annual total return and that they could therefore spend 10 percent or more of the endowment's value each year without harm. When the stock market declined in the 1960s, these enthusiasts fell victim to their own strategies. Total return rates turned negative in some cases. Institutions then found themselves spending 10 to 15 percent per year of the market value of their endowment to support current operations. Out of that painful experience came a fresh realization of the need for a new conceptual approach.

The key to the new approach was to focus on rates of change, as had been done with operating budgets. The first priority was to maintain the purchasing power of the endowment so that it did not erode with inflation. Maintaining the purchasing power meant balancing the total rate of return on the endowment principal with the rate at which funds could be paid out for operating support. While institutions now differ somewhat in the ways in which they express the rules, most now have a formula with the following components: a goal for total rate of return over time of something on the order of 10 to 12 percent per year, a payout rate amounting usually to about 5 percent that is fixed as a proportion of the market value of the endowment over some period (or that must stay within a narrow range of that relationship to endowment), and a 5 to 7 percent retention of the balance of the total return as an offset against the effects of inflation.

However, most institutions realized that it was not enough just to maintain the purchasing power of the endowment. Institutional budgets tend to grow over time, and a payout that is constant in real dollars will shrink over time in the proportion of the budget that it will support. If an endowment is to maintain its leverage for the institution (let alone increase in leverage), it must grow in real terms at least as fast as the institution's budget does. Therefore, most institutions carry on continuing vigorous campaigns to attract new capital funds to their endowment.

In summary, maintaining the leverage of endowment assets requires both a strategy for maintaining the endowment's current purchasing power and a strategy for increasing principal at least at the same rate as the institution is growing.

**Bringing the First and Second Components Together**

The analogy between the strategy for maintaining the leverage of endowment assets and a possible strategy for maintaining the leverage of plant assets may now become clear. The first challenge in the plant asset area is plant upkeep—keeping up the current value of the physical plant. The funding needed to meet that challenge can be estimated using the facility subsystem approach outlined earlier. The second challenge is plant renewal—adapting and expanding the plant to meet the evolving needs of the institution. Figure 1 contrasts the equilibrium approach to endowment asset management and plant asset management with the traditional approaches to those areas.

**Third Component of a New Theory:
Understanding Institutional Evolution**

The preceding discussion skirted the somewhat sticky issue of trying to estimate the level of plant renewal funding required to adapt the plant

**Figure 1. Traditional Versus Equilibrium Planning**

| Fund Area | Traditional Planning | Equilibrium Planning |
|---|---|---|
| Current funds | Balance annual revenues, expenditures, and transfers. | Balance growth rates of revenue, expenditure, and transfer items. |
| Endowment | Pay out only what is earned. | Purchasing power: Balance investment policy and spending rule. |
| | | Endowment leverage: Add to principal so that payout is steady or an increasing fraction of current fund expenditures. |
| Plant | Spend as needed to fix observed problems. | Plant upkeep: With systems life cycle approach, keep up existing plant for current use. |
| | | Plant renewal: Renovate and replace facilities to retain value of plant and adapt to changing institutional needs. |

to the institution's evolving mission. Two tactics, taken together, may be helpful here.

Many of the college or university's changing needs will be met through changes in its existing plant—bringing laboratories up to new standards, converting present buildings to different uses, and the like. An estimate of the likely future level of expenditures can be made by identifying plant adaption projects in recent years and basing projections of future needs on senior management judgments as to whether that level is likely to rise or fall.

The balance of the institution's evolving needs will be met through new construction. Again, a survey of recent new construction should be made. Where a new facility is a net addition to the building stock, its subsystem upkeep and renewal needs are likewise a net addition. Where a facility replaces an earlier one, the increment of its subsystem renewal and upkeep costs over those of the predecessor building are a net addition. Again, senior management should make a judgment as to whether the current level of new construction and facility replacement is likely to rise or fall, and the data for prior years can be adjusted accordingly for the new projection.

The sum of the likely future needs from new uses for existing plant and from new construction constitutes the projection amount that should be incorporated into the plant renewal category as a supplement to the plant upkeep funds. Expressed as a percentage of current plant replacement value, the amount needed for plant renewal is likely to be from 0.5 percent to 1.5 percent, depending on the character of the institution's mission (as reflected in the mix of types of its facilities) and the rapidity of technological or mission change anticipated.

Together, these flows of funds should provide a pool sufficient over the long run to pay for the cost of maintaining the leverage of plant assets on the evolving mission of the institution. The sum of the 1.5 to 2.5 percent of current plant replacement value likely to be needed to keep the plant in good condition and the 0.5 to 1.5 percent likely to be needed to adapt it to changing needs means that institutions may well be confronted with a need to provide funds in the range of 2 to 4 percent of plant replacement value each year. Figure 2 provides a simplified example of these calculations for a hypothetical three-building institution.

**Fourth Component of a New Theory:**
**Separating Accumulation and Expenditure of Funds**

Thus far, the discussion of ways of estimating the needed level of funding has not related that funding level either to sources of funding or to expenditure patterns. One significant benefit of the new approach to endowment asset management discussed in the preceding section was that it broke the overall task into three definable components and allowed one individual to be responsible for each component: The investment manager was responsible for realizing the targeted total rate of return, the development officer was responsible for finding the new capital, and the chief budget officer knew with security what level of funding he could count on for current operations. A parallel benefit can come from the approach to the preservation of the value of plant assets suggested here: The institution's chief financial officer can be responsible for the accumulation of the pool of funds, and the chief plant officer can be responsible for the expenditure on specific projects.

In the model that I am suggesting, there are a number of streams that can and should feed the total pool of funds—the annual 2 to 4 percent of total plant replacement cost. Of course, the principal source of funding should be current operating revenues: use allowances from grant and contract indirect cost reimbursement, designated endowment income and designated gifts, and an allocation from unrestricted revenues, such as tuition, state appropriations, auxiliary enterprises, unrestricted gifts, and the like. Philosophically, it seems appropriate that the current users of the physical plant should be responsible for carrying the costs of keeping

# Figure 2. Pro Forma Model of Plant Upkeep and Renewal Funding Calculation
## (in thousands of dollars)

| | | | | | | | | |
|---|---|---|---|---|---|---|---|---|
| *Calculation of Upkeep Funding Provision* | | | | *Calculation of Renewal Funding Provision* | | | | |
| Facility Subsystem | Useful Life | Current Replacement Cost | Upkeep Funding Provision[a] | Plant Changes in Last Five Years and Cost | Renewal Costs per Year[b] | Estimate of Typical Year[c] | Renewal Funding Provision[d] | Total Provision, Upkeep, and Renewal[e] |
| **Campus Center** | | | | | | | | |
| Structure | | $ 4,000 | $ 0 | | | | | |
| Interior finishes | 6 | 500 | 83 | | | | | |
| Plumbing | 50 | 750 | 15 | | | | | |
| HVAC moving | 15 | 750 | 50 | | | | | |
| | | 6,000 | 148 | | | | | |
| **Classroom and Office Building** | | | | | | | | |
| Structure | | 7,250 | 0 | Air conditioning installed, $1,000 | | | | |
| Interior finishes | 12 | 600 | 50 | | | | | |
| Plumbing | 50 | 800 | 16 | | | | | |
| HVAC moving | 15 | 1,000 | 67 | | | | | |
| | | 9,650 | 133 | | | | | |
| **Science Laboratories** | | | | | | | | |
| Structure | | 7,000 | 0 | Hoods brought to new standard, $850 | | | | |
| Interior finishes | 12 | 1,000 | 83 | | | | | |
| Plumbing | 30 | 1,500 | 50 | | | | | |
| HVAC moving | 12 | 1,850 | 154 | | | | | |
| | | 11,350 | 288 | | | | | |
| Totals | | $27,000 | $569 | $1,850 | $370 | 80% | $296 | $865 |
| Percent of total plant replacement cost | | | 2.1% | | | | 1.1% | 3.2% |

[a]Replacement cost divided by useful life.
[b]Total five-year renewal costs divided by 5.
[c]Estimate from senior management.
[d]Annual costs times "typical year" estimate.
[e]Sum of upkeep and renewal provisions.

the plant in good current condition and for supplying the plant upkeep funding component. To adapt the plant to new uses, it makes sense to look to sources other than current users. Capital fund-raising and designated state appropriations are likely to be the main sources. It is recognized that the specific sources of funding that are possible and appropriate as constituents of the overall pool will vary considerably among types of institution, depending on their financial structure and control. In this model, the chief financial officer is responsible for estimating the size of the annual contribution to the plant asset upkeep-and-renewal pool and for procuring and setting aside that level of funding each year.

In contrast, the chief plant officer is responsible for identifying the plant projects that are needed in a systematic way over time and for managing them. The projects will be paid for out of the overall pool of funds. The advantage of this arrangement is that the dollars needed for specific projects will vary from year to year. So long as the flow of funds into the pool is regular and sufficient, shocks to the operating budgets can be avoided even though annual drawdowns vary in size. A second advantage is that the chief plant officer can plan facility projects several years into the future, knowing that the pool of funding needed will be there.

**Transition to a New Approach**

Few if any institutions of higher education in the United States are putting amounts aside for plant upkeep and renewal as high as those called for in this model. That is one reason why the APPA/NACUBO study (Rush, 1988) found that correcting the urgent needs—maintenance items that cause the facility to be at risk if they are not done—to be approximately $20 billion and that the aggregate deferred maintenance in colleges and universities reached an appalling $60 to $70 billion. We have created this situation for ourselves by underfunding plant upkeep and renewal. Another way of saying this is that we have allowed the value of our collective college and university plant assets to erode by that amount.

It is difficult to change the funding base for a higher education institution in a hurry. When universities began to adopt the new approach to endowment asset protection, many found that it took five to ten years to reduce the drawdown rates on endowment to sustainable levels. Had they reduced the drawdown rates more precipitately, they would have forced severe cutbacks in operating budgets.

It will be correspondingly difficult for institutions to adopt the approach to facility upkeep and renewal funding described here. At my own institution, Tufts University, we have raised the plant upkeep and renewal funding about 20 percent per year over and above inflation for five straight years in an attempt to bring it up to an appropriate level, but we still have a long way to go. As a new approach is developed to the point where it can easily be applied, the application is almost necessarily going to involve using the concept for many years to identify the amount that should be put aside, while the actual level of inflow to the pool is raised gradually to that level.

In the meantime, it seems critically important to avoid a common mistake. Many institutions have conducted extensive facilities audits, identified a list of major projects, and borrowed money to undertake those projects—without providing that the repayment of that debt must be over and above the funds needed to continue keeping the plant in shape. Unless they do so, they may be spending now to fix up plant neglected in the past, but they are creating a similar or worse situation for themselves in the future.

## Further Development of the New Theory

A project team led by the Society for College and University Planning, in association with the Association of Physical Plant Administrators of Colleges and Universities, the National Association of College and University Business Officers, and the accounting firm of Coopers & Lybrand has begun to work toward a clarification and refinement of these ideas, in hopes of arriving at a conceptual approach that all four partners agree on and can advocate for use.

## References

Association of Physical Plant Administrators of Colleges and Universities, National Association of Colleges and University Business Officers, and Coopers & Lybrand. *The Decaying American Campus: A Ticking Time Bomb*. Alexandria, Va.: Association of Physical Plant Administrators of Colleges and Universities, 1989.

Dunn, J. A., Jr., and Sonenstein, B. S. "Plant Upkeep and Financial Equilibrium: What Does It Take to Stay in Balance?" In *Proceedings of the Northeast Association for Institutional Research Annual Conference*. 1986

Flanagan, J. S. "How to Attain a Healthy Physical Plant." *Business Officer*, March 1983, p. 28.

Helpern, D. P. *The State of College and University Facilities*. New York: Society for College and University Planning, 1987.

Hopkins, D.S.P., and Massy, W. F. *Planning Models for Colleges and Universities*. Stanford, Calif.: Stanford University Press, 1981.

Hutson, R. E., and Biedenweg, F. M. "Before the Roof Caves In: A Predictive Model for Physical Plant Renewal." *APPA Newsletter*, July 1982, pp. 7-10; August 1982, pp. 7-12.

Kaiser, H. H. "Funding of Facility Repairs and Renovation." *Business Officer*, January 1982, pp. 22-24.

Kaiser, H. H. *Crumbling Academe*. Washington, D.C.: Association of Governing Boards, 1984.

Kaiser, H. H. *Facilities Audit Workbook.* Alexandria, Va.: Association of Physical Plant Administrators of Colleges and Universities, 1987.

National Science Foundation. *Scientific and Engineering Research Facilities at Universities and Colleges: 1988.* Washington, D.C.: National Science Foundation, 1988.

Rush, S. Remarks at the press conference of the Association of Physical Plant Administrators and the National Association of College and University Business Officers, Washington, D.C., October 13, 1988.

Wyatt, J. B., Emery, J. C., and Landis, C. P., (eds.). *Financial Planning Models: Concepts and Case Studies in Colleges and Universities.* Princeton, N.J.: EDUCOM, 1979.

*John A. Dunn, Jr., is vice-president of planning, Tufts University.*

# Index